BLACK ENTERPRISE
IN BRITAIN

By Tony Wade
with a Foreword by Dr. Roselle Antoine

1

Cover designed by Wiseworks Enterprises

Production by Wiseworks Enterprises

Printed by Wiseworks Enterprises

First Published October 2003
Second Edition May 2005

ISBN 0-9542325-3-4 (Pb)

Other Publications by the Author
"How they made a Million"

ISBN 18705-18837 (Pb)

Black Enterprise In Britain

Dedication

Dedicated to all those people
who have made Black Enterprise in Britain possible

The researcher, author and publisher have exercised great care in ensuring that everything included in this publication is accurate. The intent is to give a fair and broad picture of black development and we unreservedly apologise for any unintentional inaccuracy.

The publisher unreservedly apologises to all purchasers for inadvertent publishing errata in the first edition, which has now been withdrawn and recycled.

Daphne

Acknowledgements

I have been honoured in having a number of students who, in writing their thesis, have taken time to interview me at length about my business career as material worthy to write about.

It was arising out of these interviews that I was urged, for sake of posterity, to jot down my thoughts on the contributions made by black and Caribbean peoples in general to the economic life of Britain. They urged the need for a base line, a yardstick by which future generations can measure black progress.

Over the last two decades the significance of black history month has gained in importance, and infused a spirit of community pride and self-esteem. The more we can talk about progress and cherish our hard won achievements, the more we ought to foster and keep on winning goals for the community and the nation.

It is with this in mind that I attempt to identify some areas of progress and, in doing so, pay special tribute to all those mentioned in these pages, who are the true heroes in making this work possible.

I am indebted to Dr Christopher Johnson for carrying out much of the research making this book possible, to Margaret Alexander for the proof reading, and to journalist Robert Govender for his much valued advice.

This work could not have been completed without the patient, kind and indulgent support of my darling wife Vasantha, and the encouragement of my children, Samenua Sesher, Sarah and Aqasa Nu, along with Philip and Olga Try, who together have been a major source of strength and inspiration.

Contents

Introduction

This book does not purport to include the whole raft of black contribution and entrepreneurial activity in the U K - this would be virtually an impossible task. Rather, it highlights some areas of activity and gives a broad picture of the black community's hard work showing how, through its own efforts, it is gradually adding value to the nation's economic base, increasing productivity, employment, and wealth creation.

It is in part a historical document, capturing some aspects of our past achievements. It looks at our current engagement, and our vision for the future. Without a past there could be no present, without the present there can be no future. Black Enterprise must be seen in its widest possible context, embracing the gamut of human endeavour, a priceless resource of effort and energy which reflects a more measured and meaningful responsiveness to society as a whole. Each chapter, therefore, looks beyond purely pounds and pence, incorporating our human capital investment in the UK economy. This book sums up, therefore, our contribution to the nation's wealth creation.

Britain is today a multicultural country, the most colourful and cosmopolitan nation in all Europe. Her history and traditions make her a magnet for the intake of a rich mixture of cultures which blend into a remarkable melting pot which is the envy of the world. Each wave of immigrants has enriched the cultural and social fabric of British society, and represents building blocks of prosperity.

West Indians have, for example, given Britain Carnival, the largest street festival in Europe. Carnival's output of glitter is stress releasing in character and a real tonic for people who lead a busy life, for the young and old alike. The event has demonstrated tremendous creativity, energy and sheer brilliance by producers and revellers alike. Carnival also has created a range of enterprises, not forgetting its huge contribution to Britain's tourist industry.

It has also transplanted its cool and enchanting array of colours loved and worn by the fashion conscious. It has also delivered its music in a variety of exciting rhythms, bubbling with enchantment - of sun, sea and sand, rhythms that make you always want to dance. Bob Marley's Reggae Gospel with its infectious messages of love and peace was voted the song of the twentieth Century. Steel band music is now a recognised art form loved and enjoyed nationally. Unfamiliar and delightful dishes now abound, eschoveitch fish, red snappers, ackee and salt fish, rice and peas, patties, roties and a host of others for ones eating pleasure.

Food flavourings which make Caribbean cooking a delight are plentiful and now sought after in Britain. Jerk seasoning brings out the flavour in meats and fish and no barbecue is ever complete without its addition. It is available at most supermarkets. Some Caribbean restaurants now offer a choice of jerked pork, chicken and fish, and it will not be long before we see jerk fast food chains.

An assortment of root vegetables and fruits abound, varieties of yam, dasheen, breadfruit, chou-chou and sweet potatoes, to name but a few, while in the fruit range, mangoes are plentiful, sweet sop and sour sop, naseberries and oranges. In the orange family, the ortanique scores as the most desirable for its fleshy pulp and plentiful juice rich in vitamin C.

Caribbean rums made famous by the buccaneers are known the world over. We think of Captain Morgan, Appleton Reserve and Cockspur, to name a few, reputed for making the spirits fly. It is said that *"when the spirit is in, the man is out."* Tropical thirst quenchers in flavours galore compete for shelf space while Red Stripe, the leading lager of the Caribbean, has carved out a respectable share for itself in the UK market.

The terms West Indian and Caribbean used in this book are interchangeable. West Indian represents part of our colonial legacy which informs on all aspects of our identity. The use of Caribbean, on the other hand, is symbolic of a modern regional nation of peoples tied to a common destiny. When I set out to research and write this book, I did so with a feeling of optimism, a strong faith in the ability of my fellow West Indians to consolidate and build on the modest, hard won, material, spiritual and commercial gains made ever since their migration to this country from the late forties onwards.

To be sure, there were some worrying statistics about the prejudice and discrimination they encountered in practically every walk of life. This information came not only from the race relations industry and independent research units, but also from government, especially the Home Office. It is not generally the practice of governments to admit their mistakes: they always try to cover up. But in the race relations area, under Tony Blair, the Prime Minister and Jack Straw, the past Home Secretary, there has been open acknowledgement that minorities do not get a fair deal.

Perhaps the most historic event of all was the resounding indictment of

British institutional racism by Lord McPherson, who headed the Stephen Lawrence Inquiry. His recommendations shook all right-minded people. Institutional racism, he boldly stated, was not only widespread in the police but in most areas of British life. To its credit, the Blair government welcomed McPherson's findings and must be congratulated on its decision to set up the inquiry in the first place. The Inquiry represented a courageous and revolutionary act, unprecedented in the troubled history of race relations in this country.

However, it did not stop there. Home Secretary Jack Straw's instructions to the police to recruit 8,000 extra ethnic minority police is indicative of the serious determination of New Labour to take practical measures to speed up the advance towards a more acceptable multicultural society. New Labour has put in motion a number of initiatives to involve the community in the reshaping of British society, a most welcome development.

It was a depressing message for that small minority like the nail bombers, the men of hate and violence. These desperate people hoped that their violent reaction would frighten and divide our nation and sabotage efforts to peacefully transform our society.

There was great fear and anxiety in the gay, Asian, African-Caribbean and African communities. These communities, which have been subjected to violence and harassment, are familiar with the objective of the far-right, which actually believes that it can terrorise the ethnic minorities into fleeing this country. These communities refuse to be intimidated. They believe that this is their country too. This belief is strongest among minority youth.

However, Tony Blair, already a statesman of world stature, added further to his laurels when he boldly and unhesitatingly nailed his colours to the anti-racist mast. He means business when he says that those who seek to divide the communities will be defeated. Addressing a meeting of the Sikh community in Birmingham on May 3 1999, the Prime Minister launched a powerful attack on the nail bombers. He told the Sikhs, and through them the wider community, that there was a direct parallel between the fight to defeat " *injustice and intolerance at home* " with Nato's battle against ethnic cleansing in Kosovo. The values were the same he reassured his audience. When one section of our community is under attack, we defend them in the name of all the community. When bombers attack the black and Asian communities in Britain, they attack the whole of Britain. When the gay community is attacked and innocent people are murdered, all the good people of Britain, whatever their race, their lifestyle, their class, unite in revulsion and determination to bring the evil people to justice."

Patriotism in Britain no longer excluded people because of their colour, religion or ethnic background. Blair said he took pride in diversity which *"enriches and unites"* the country. And he added, *"the true outcasts of today, the true minorities, those truly excluded are not the different races and religions of Britain, but the racists, the bombers, the violent criminals who hate the vision of Britain and try to destroy it. But they shall not win. The great decent majority of British people will not let them. We will defeat them. We will defeat them and then we can build the tolerant multicultural Britain the vast majority of us want to see."*

The Prime Minister faced up to another reality, acknowledging that the Stephen Lawrence case showed that Britain still had a long way to go before achieving the vision of a truly multiracial society, but adding *" we can take hope from the distance already travelled."*

This was, perhaps, the most resounding affirmation yet of Britain's unflinching commitment to the establishment of a just multicultural society, coming as it has from the leader of the nation.

I have been particularly touched by what the Prime Minister had to say, as it has been a subject that I personally have been urging all along, and quote from a speech that I made in Manchester on 23rd May 1985:

" I have over the years been connected to various organisations, whose noble objectives are to bring about a more equitable and a more just society, by the fostering of good and harmonious relations, and have always contended that here in Britain we have the best opportunity of holding up a model to the rest of the world.

Our capacity for tolerance, caring and understanding, the major ingredients, are unsurpassed anywhere else, and are qualities which we must collectively not hesitate in bringing to bear on the needs of members of communities less fortunate than ourselves, particularly through no fault of their own."

The media, quite often silent or ambiguous in the face of racist outrage, was also united in its revulsion against the nail bombers. Perhaps the best media retort to the men of violence came from the Sunday Times newspaper, one of the largest Sunday papers, being so forceful in its defence of civilised values. This was a source of enormous comfort to the beleaguered gay and ethnic minority communities.

Normally, the multicultural message is the monopoly of the liberal, small and left-leaning press in this country, which, though well meaning, preaches largely to the converted. Under the heading, *Dangerous Times,* the Sunday Times presented the case for zero tolerance towards the wreckers and saboteurs:

"Britain no longer seems quite the safe and tolerant place we believed it to be. Three fanatical bombings and the senseless murder of a much loved television personality have shattered some illusions. Racial violence of the sort that has killed three people and injured more than 120 in the past two weeks harks back to the Nazis, who found little support in Britain beyond the Mosleyites. We have to face the fact that the mindless extremism that has shattered innocent lives in London's Soho, Brick Lane and Brixton does exist on the outer fringes of our society and its proponents are prepared to murder and maim almost indiscriminately." And the paper goes on; *"The government, police and security services must use all their resources to ensure that those who despise civilised behaviour must pay for it."*

In this book, I have dealt at length with the artistic, aesthetic, musical, satirical, and fashion influence of our communities on British life. Reggae is one example of the great exports of the Caribbean. Reggae is no longer a Caribbean monopoly. It is claimed by the youth of Europe as their very own. Now it has a more universal ownership as the following report under the witty heading, *"Brixton beat fills the street of Algiers"* (a despatch from the capital of Algeria) in the British liberal daily. The Guardian of May 6,1999 shows: " In the smoky dives known as les bars, the disaffected young men of Algiers gather to drink, talk and listen to live music. But close your eyes for a second and you could be forgiven for imagining you were in South London. Blended with rai music are reggae baselines. "Reggae Islam" has taken off in the Algerian capital. The inspiration comes not from Jamaica, but Brixton where " Reggae Islam" is said to be thriving."

This book seeks to recapture from where we have come, our accomplishments, and our contribution to a more inclusive and enlightened society.

It looks to the brighter side of life and stems from the conviction that Britain is a fundamentally decent society, that the rule of law will always prevail, and as Tony Blair reminded us, while we still have a long way to go before achieving the vision of a truly tolerant society, *"we can take hope in the distance travelled."*

The following pages are thus markers and milestones of the community's journeying.

Foreword

Nothing is more important to a people's development than its pursuits to document its place in society, and in this particular context, it is that of the fabric of British History. As with the Author's first book, "How they made a Million", this volume is a first and perfect example of the plethora of Black achievement among individuals and organizations in a way which dispels the myth about our lack of a business culture.

"Black Enterprise in Britain" embodies developmental issues, including education, law, literature, politics, the media, religion, and sport, to name a few. It is an invaluable contribution and tribute to those who have struggled to make a definitive impact on the tapestry of British society, and as such, it has succeeded in enlarging our understanding of our place in society in Britain, as well as creating an indelible mark on Black enterprise development in the Diaspora.

The Black enterprise talent is one of our most valuable resources. It is needed now, at a time when "positive role-modelling for our youths" is being clamoured for in our 21st Century. This book sets the records straight, and leaves the reader in no doubt that from an educational point of view, its effectiveness is unlimited; in the classroom, for teachers, mentors, families, the student, social workers, the probation and prison service, and researchers alike, and cannot be underplayed.

Overall, this volume therefore assists in the dissemination of the fruits of black enterprise or entrepreneurship, scholarship, culture, economic independence, and presents one of the liveliest engagements of economic success, in a worthy process of nation building.

Dr. Roselle Antoine

Preface

Black Enterprise in Britain is an overdue initiative. Often we find that the contribution of black peoples in Britain has been reduced to token gestures. One classic example is the celebration of Black History Month in October since 1987 (when this occasion was borrowed from Black America) - to highlight the work of Black communities in the country. Yet most of the activities tend to reflect a cultural and sporting bias.

Tony Wade's spirited effort to capture sequences of the black contribution to British society is therefore hugely commendable at this juncture. In documenting the contribution of black peoples to British society, the author presents a mixture of semi-biographical and part-historical essays, along with useful anecdotes of enterprise, to demonstrate the achievements among African and Caribbean communities.

As a chronicler of black enterprise development, Wade writes from an excellent position, having been a successful entrepreneur for the past 40 years in Britain. His appointment to several high profile public bodies also makes him an authority on the subject. His wide-ranging recommendations, apart from being opportune, also reveal a real sense of urgency, especially since the black contribution to corporate Britain is integral to national economic policy. By making this work accessible, Wade has redefined too, black peoples' place in British history, if not in the world. In effect, he has redrawn the contours of debate on what really constitutes the black presence in modern Britain.

It is hoped that this book, which is ideal for students, researchers, policy makers, entrepreneurs and the wider public, will go a far way in presenting an accurate picture of black British history rather than the perpetual and worn script accepted as the norm. Moreover, it will inspire confidence and renewal regarding a better understanding of the makings of a multicultural nation such as Britain.

Dr. Christopher A. Johnson

Small Business & Enterprise

Small businesses are quite often the engine for expanding economic activity and, in the African and Caribbean context, this is the scenario that most certainly applies.

Enterprise in Britain by the African Caribbean community has its roots in its cultural activities. This route is not dissimilar to that followed by other ethnic groupings. The last few decades have seen huge movements in migration, fuelled in the main by a combination of push/supply and pull/demand factors. This will continue even more so, stimulated by economic globalisation made possible by the revolutions in communication and transport.

I am confident in sounding a positive note that the black business community is breaking out of the stagnation in which it has had to suffer disproportionate pain and suffering in getting heard, let alone making it onto a level playing field.

The media circulated a perception, which gained widespread currency, that black owned business was all bad business, without carefully examining each case and dealing with it on merit. The banking system too purports, by its actions, to give credence to this perception by dismally failing to publicly disprove the claims levelled against them for failing to support black businesses fairly.

It would be of immense help to the reader to look briefly at the historic background which would give a clear picture of some of the many odds that were stacked against the early immigrants to fully understand why emerging black businesses found the going so tough.

The vast majority of immigrants that came to Britain during the fifties and sixties were economic refugees coming mainly from an agricultural background lacking in industrial skills.

There were, however, a number of trades people with skills in construction, carpentry, engineering and motor mechanical repair, shop fitters, painters, tailors and dressmakers etc. Skilled persons in these categories had little choice to work in their specialist areas, and were forced to take menial poor paying jobs, which hampered capital accumulation.

In addition, most emigrating families were split up, with fathers coming first, leaving mothers and children and the extended family behind, which meant losing their immediate support system, the back bone of any community.

These splintered family structures caused terrible dislocation and, combined with poor pay, racial abuse, homelessness and countless other social burdens, placed the Caribbean community at a major disadvantage. It therefore has taken much longer to build new supporting structures to compete effectively with other groups in the society.

From the foregoing it is clear to see how limitations on the community impacted on black business development within the society by putting their businesses at a disadvantage right from the start.

The white owned banking establishments are the same people who owned the large plantations in the Caribbean and were not prepared to take risks with businesses with whom they could not relate in the same manner as they could with their own kith and kin, even in situations where bank support entailed no risk.

Let us look at two other examples of immigrant groupings which put the picture in perspective.

The Cypriot community dominates the clothing industry both in manufacturing, fashion and design. They came with the necessary skills and had the full support of an extended family which supported the development of their industry and its expansion into the wider community. With the home market pocketed, they were poised to move into export markets. Furthermore, Cypriot banks emerged providing the financial support their businesses needed to expand.

The East African Asian community came with both business skills and wealth that they had accumulated and were able to invest and engage in a variety of businesses in the mainstream of the society. Thus they were able to take advantage of the economy of scale that the mainstream provided. They too, had the benefit of their own banking systems, which further helped to consolidate their position in the market place.

The Caribbean business community had no such starts, and therefore lagged behind at the bottom of the pile, having to fight every step of the way to get its voice heard with little or no response from officialdom and the powers in control. It took riots borne out of hardship and despair for the Conservative Government of the day to wake up to the dangers of neglect.

Lord Scarman's enquiry into the riots outlined accurately, the problems faced by the black community's small businesses.

His report and recommendations were accepted by the Thatcher government, which implemented some of the recommendations, which went some way in an attempt to address some of the problems.

The report was universally hailed, for it echoed exactly what organisations such as the UK Caribbean Chamber of Commerce have been putting forward all along. Below is a quote from the report:

"The encouragement of black people to secure a real stake in their community, through business and the professions, is of great importance if future social stability is to be secured - I do urge the necessity for speedy action if we are to avoid the perpetuation in this country of an economically dispossessed black population."

The spirit of enterprise has always been an inherent part of the community's make up. It was this very spirit which, in the first place, led most people to emigrate to Britain in search of improving their social condition.

For many, addressing some of their social ills of poor pay and racial injustice, taking the self employment route and being prepared to work hard was one way to a better future.

Enterprising black ambition is no guesswork. Home Office statistics show that black business start up is the highest of all groups, proof enough of the community's desire for independence and self-determination.

West Indians, on the whole, have innate enterprise skills. They have been survivors in environments where welfare was not always available, and the instinct for survival drives people with ambition who value their independence and do something about it.

It is a fact that the African Caribbean population, unlike the Asians, have made little progress in the retail sector - in corner shops and general stores. To the Asians' credit, they have been very successful at providing goods and services consumed, to a large extent, by black customers.

A question that is commonly asked time and time over is "Why are there not more blacks in this area of business?" The answer is simple, in that the Asians spotted an opportunity and had the resources to take advantage of it for reasons already mentioned. While they dominate this area of trading, it is not exclusive. It would also be true in mentioning that a culture exists in their community which allows a round the clock service to be provided which other ethnic groups are unable or unwilling to perform.

The government's immigration policy in the early fifties was aimed at meeting the demands of labour shortages, especially in the health service and transport sectors. High unemployment in the West Indies immediately after the Second World War, and the opportunity to find work in Britain was welcomed with open arms. Many people who migrated to the United Kingdom had planned on returning home after a short period.

Apart from the skilled and unskilled, professional people in various other disciplines also followed, which amounted to a brain drain on the region. After independence West Indian governments sought to reverse the brain drain, but the lure of being better rewarded abroad was too great to resist. The loss of civil servants in particular had a marked affect on implementing some government policies.

Despite the many set backs referred to earlier, the dogged determination of business people has at last started to take its place in the economic life of the nation, breaking out of purely ethnic markets which limits room for growth.

The first hub of sole traders and family businesses flourished, especially in Brixton. The community, mostly Jamaicans, were sufficiently highly motivated and large enough to sustain a growing demand for the goods and services needed by the community.

From the sixties onwards Brixton's dynamism and its bustling enterprises have continued to grow and is a great credit to the people of the area. They attracted patronage from near and far. Its unique environs too, have become far more pleasurable for shopping. Its welcome and friendliness added to its attraction for customers.

Brixton is today gentrified and dominated by West Indian pubs where patrons meet to socialise and discuss business. George Berry, a well-known raconteur, owned the Coach and Horses, while Tony Waller ran the Enterprise on Coldharbour Lane.

The town of Brixton could quite easily be described as the Black Capital of London. The area houses a good mix of all the features of a friendly and loveable town and has had more exposure (perhaps some for the wrong reasons) than any other thickly black populated area in the UK.

Independent Television used this venue to give coverage to Lambeth Central Parliamentary Bye-election in 1978. Lloyd Leon, mime host at the Atlantic, a central point for the black community, became Mayor of Lambeth and has since acquired Mingles restaurant/pub - a delightful retreat for relaxation.

The late L.E. Campbell & Son became a household name. He pioneered the group travel industry from 3, Vining Street which for years moved thousands of people to and from the Caribbean under the banner of (JOFFA), the Jamaican Families & Friends Association. Black Brixtonians are a proud, energetic, outgoing and cheerful lot, credited for spear heading the first black community businesses.

Names that have left an indelible mark on the Brixton landscape include, Columbus Fabrics, and Martyn's Cosmetics and of course LE Campbell & Son.

These pages will show how African Caribbean people rose to the challenges of the market place carving out, through dedication and hard work, their own employment generating machinery in sectors of businesses inside the mainstream as distinct from traditional ethnic cultural operations, which placed limitations on growth.

Up the road from Brixton in Balham, could be found Howard Baugh & Sons Ltd, a Jamaican family owned and run company that exhibited all the hallmarks of a good professionally managed organisation. The company's businesses are noteworthy.

It was the first black community company to land car dealerships, first with the Chrysler Corporation (Europe) and next with the Mazda Corporation of Japan. Among the company's other remarkable exploits were petrol distribution franchises from Mobil Oil for a number of petrol stations it owned. Garage operations also formed part of the company's operations.

Howard Baugh is a man gifted with a towering presence and financial mental agility. His business acumen spans other areas, notably as shareholder and chairman of the capital's largest black owned radio station, CHOICE FM. He gave generously of his time as Chairman of (UK) Caribbean Chamber of Commerce.

CHOICE FM is a flagship of black enterprise - the face and voice of black London in radio and the pride of the public it serves.

Its offices and operations centre are housed in a ten thousand square feet freehold building it owns at 291/299 Borough High Street S.E.1, a stone's throw from the city. This prime location is reportedly valued at around £4/5 million while the business itself has a current market value in the region of £20/25 million.

Opportunity, I have always argued, is the key for freeing up the entrepreneurial spirit of the community and allowing it to make its presence felt. Trickling down has been the age-old code which slows up the economic progress of our people. Examples of this trickle down can be cited as follows. The BBC's brief spot for Black Londoners, hosted by Alex Pascall was summarily killed off despite its immense popularity. So too, was Sid Burke's "Rice & Peas" which suffered the same fate.

Trickling down prevents the products provider from being masters in their own right, fenced in as it were. Choice's break through out of this bind is a cause for rejoicing at the end of a solid campaign of hard work. The station is a major landmark in presenting original black musical culture and a positive in the development of a range of skills and talents that would never have seen the light of day without the station. The community salutes the pioneering spirit of Patrick Berry, Neil Kinlock and Howard Baugh. The city could never be the same again, without Choice FM.

Another Black enterprising first in its field came from Jamaican Stewart Weathers with his novel introduction of Help Plumbing Ltd, a twenty-four hour service around London that revolutionised the plumbing business.

His business was so successful that it spawned an army of followers that copied his formula. Quite apart from providing Weathers with just rewards for being visionary, it delivered to the capital city a long neglected round the clock service which was well received by its residents.

Stewart's life style was the envy of many of his peer group. He lived like an aristocrat with memberships of several elite clubs, including the Playboy and the Park Lane Casino Club. He enjoyed flying light aircraft, horse riding and collecting paintings.

Joy Nichols is owner and Chief Executive of Nichols Employment Agency, one of the community's foremost female entrepreneurs. Her management skills are quite remarkable and have earned her enormous respect from all sections of society.

Her story is all the more intriguing in that she conceived her business idea of setting up her Agency while lying on her back giving birth to her baby. Like most successful people she translated her idea from her living room with little or no capital (£100) into a £5 million company today.

Nichols Training Ltd is a subsidiary of Nichols Employment Agency. It specialises in providing quality training with linkages across further education colleges in North West London, which dovetails neatly into a work placement arrangement that serves the community well. Delivery of NVQ training in Care and Bespoke Specialist training for black and ethnic minorities is a most welcome development.

Well deserved credits and awards to this super lady come from a number of well-known organisations. These include the Federation of Black Women Business Owners, the Voice Newspaper, and the London Focus Group. Her organisation memberships are many including Middlesex University Business School Advisory Committee, the Metropolitan Police Task Force

Partnership Committee and Chair of the African/Caribbean Business Network.

The Voice is today, Britain's leading black weekly newspaper with a circulation figure of around fifty thousand copies weekly.

As the title suggests, it is the "VOICE" of the black community. Founded in 1982 by the late Val Mc Calla in the aftermath of the Brixton riots, it accurately reflected the frustrations and bitterness arising mainly out of political neglect, which the rioters were voicing.

Unlike other black publications, its target readership was aimed at the young upwardly mobile black Britons, the second generation who were not prepared to accept and endure second-rate treatment as their forebears. The paper enjoyed a groundswell of popular support from its inception ensuring its immediate success. The formula was simple enough, the paper conveyed the views and aspirations of its readership and they supported the paper.

Knightway, a well-respected publication in the fields of recruitment, retention and employer communications, carried out a joint survey with The Voice. I quote from the survey:

" Over half the sample of 1,500 drawn from readers of The Voice do not believe they have equal promotion prospects with white colleagues. And two-thirds of men and nearly half the women said they experienced racial discrimination in their careers. John Salkeld, Director of Research and Planning for Knightway, said the results were invaluable for those concerned with equality and efficiency in recruitment and selection among an important section of Britain's ethnic minorities ".

Further, Salkeld declared, "effective equal opportunities policies are a necessity as well as an ideal. The need for changing attitudes is even more important against the background of dramatic changes in the workforce profile." The above statements are quoted, in that they echo the sentiments of what led to the founding of the paper in the first place.

In the meanwhile enlightened Borough Councils across the country, fearing trouble in their back yard, supported a policy of being more inclusive in their employment practices and made sure that their advertisements for staff were included in the publication. This was a lucky break for the paper, for not only did advertising take care of meeting its overheads, but it also increased its readership, some coming from white employers and white job seekers. The paper's comprehensive cluster of jobs turned out to be one of the best there is around.

In a fact finding survey, it was discovered that response to adverts by councils had a knock on effect in that mainstream businesses that favoured diversity saw the Voice as the best channel for some of their recruitment.

The paper's influence is far reaching. Policy makers both at the local and national levels keenly study its editorial on issues of the day. Community issues and concerns are given first-rate airing, which evokes healthy responses from its readers.

Quite apart from the employment opportunities that flow from a successful business, of equal importance also, are the skills and experiences that are produced and fed into the wider market place.

The paper's community support is visible in a multitude of ways, and to name them all is impossible, suffice to say these include scholarships and sponsorships.

The 'VOICE GROUP' was another milestone. Other titles included The 'Weekend Voice', and 'The Journal'.

Barbadian Colin Carter has played and continues to play a prominent role in the UK business life. As a past secretary of the (UK) Caribbean Chamber of Commerce, he was responsible for its renewal and growth after years of stagnation. He read sociology at Morley and City Colleges on arrival in Britain and, after a brief spell in the civil service, he founded ECCY (Barbados) and (UK) Ltd alongside Jet Load Travel Ltd, providing a number of essential services to the community.

Carter was one of the earliest businessmen to advocate that his compatriots should become more involved in commerce and industry— intensely progressive, he practices what he preaches. He is the owner of Caribbean Funeral Services, providing a dignified service to the community's departed.

The label "CHARLIE ALLEN" is the ultimate brand in men's wear. Charlie Allen senior came from Montserrat and passed on his skills to his son. The young Charlie mastered the craft and, coupled with his entrepreneurial flair, he was soon noticed at the many trade shows which he attended in New York, London and Paris. He soon became a big hitter in the business. His show room and workshop in Upper Street Islington, adjacent to the city, is the haute couture for the elite. To be seen in a "CHARLIE ALLEN" suit confirms that you have arrived.

The very discerning Japanese have admired his company's work and CHARLIE ALLEN is a popular men's brand sold across Japan today. At the last count the company's garments were in thirty-seven stores.

STATECRAFT CONSULTING Ltd is the brainchild of Rudi Page, the Managing Director. He is a second generation black Briton. His organisation is unique - it is the only black company consulting on cultural knowledge.

Driven by a very talented and highly motivated individual, the organisation has made a significant contribution to the overall economic life of Britain in a unique way by its innovative approach of focusing as it does on cultural knowledge, which has enabled a number of large organisations to acknowledge the importance of cross-cultural issues, particularly in organisation development, and service delivery.

The company has developed new strategic communication and development tools widely commended for their innovative approach to regeneration and economic development. It has a formidable track record, having worked with government departments in the UK, the USA and in the Caribbean. Other organisations to benefit from the company's services include the Royal College of Nursing, Chambers of Commerce, and other public sector bodies.

Through the company's vision, commitment and drive, cross-cultural and cross-sectoral alliances, networks and partnerships have been formed, enabling not only the integration of black businesses into the mainstream economy, but has also helped to focus a more positive view of the cultural diversity of Britain.

Community participation in the mainstream in the key sectors of manufacturing and distribution has been the declared ambition of Norman Ryan from Montserrat. He founded Woodcraft (Herts.) in 1971, manufacturing a wide range of pet products. He supplied major chain stores throughout the UK, which included such names as Harrods, Woolworths and "Wonder Pet".

Woodcraft was reported to be the largest producer of pet products made of wood, with export markets in Germany, the Netherlands and Northern Ireland.

Later he launched Bloom Ben Ltd, producing a unique wooden lampshade, which was sold in over a thousand stores including the John Lewis Partnership.

Ryan has since returned to Montserrat where he is now busily engaged in the food industry.

North London based Dr Ken Ife is an illustrious academic, and a distinguished entrepreneur.

As an academic, he holds a BSc in Industrial Chemistry, a PhD in

Mineral Engineering, an MBA in Corporate Strategy and completed post graduate study in Multinational Investment, earning him a law degree LL.M. This wealth of interrelated disciplines has equipped him for what life has thrown at him.

His entrepreneurial and innovative skills put him firmly in the forefront of black business development.

His company, Data Consultants Ltd, is at the cutting edge of technology training and filling a reported 3,000 employment places annually. As early as 1986 Dr. Ife was running as many as 50 local employment centres across London, while his subsidiary Paks Micro International is synonymous with the computer training industry across Nigeria where the company is a major player.

His skill in Industrial Chemistry has been brought to bear on his Edmonton based All Soft cosmetics manufacturing operation which produces a range of products and has opened up significant employment opportunities for local people.

All Soft's sales force is aggressively targeting the export market place, and currently exports a substantial quantity of its products into Africa.

Dr. Ife is a highly motivated, dynamic and committed black community leader. Quite apart from his phenomenal personal business successes, his leadership in community economic development is outstanding and greatly admired and respected by the many organisations with whom he works providing free consultancy.

His tireless leadership currently extends across 15 organisations where he is either Chairman or Board Member/Director. These include Business Link, the National Agency for Export Promotion. He is Chairman of Haringey Business Development Agency, Director/ Treasurer of the African/Caribbean Network, and Board Member of Haringey City Growth Strategy, to name but a few. These bodies are all engaged in strategies that determine the direction of economic policies and programmes.

His enormous contribution to Black Community development is widely recognised and greatly valued by the entire community. His generosity in cash and kind is exemplary.

MPS Destinations plc, in South London's New Cross area, promotes itself as 'the one stop shop for people going places'. This is very unusual for a company engaged in the freight industry - and it is literally so, however - for the friendly kind of shop where people can walk in off the high street and make their freight arrangements to Kingston, Bridgetown, Nairobi or wherever. New Cross is a very multi-cultural area, with a strong African and Caribbean community. A blue plastic 'barrel' container of the type used in the industry for personal shipments advertises the company's rates to a range of destinations.

The 'one stop' statement, Lobban asserts, stems from the fact that MPS also offers passenger travel, money transfer, 'tropicalised' goods such as TV's and fridges, and also a property sales, design and build service in the Caribbean.

Mark Lobban learnt the freight business where he worked previously as freight manager for a UK company, and started his own operation in the early 1980's from a small business centre in Greenwich, and experienced all the start-up pains that new businesses go through, particularly during the early nineties recession. He puts the success of MPS down to hard work, a dogged determination and by offering the best possible service to the company's customers.

It is very much a family affair, with his wife running his accounts department and his brother managing the shipping operation.

"Developing a young business" he says, "and particularly a young black business, is not easy. My bank manager often tells me that we have to be better than the rest. People tend to scrutinise us harder because of the colour of our skin, asking: 'Can we trust you with our worldly goods?' and that applies equally from people of my own community as well as from everyone else".

"This is a very tight market", he explains. "Most of the big international removals operators do not get involved in the Caribbean because of this factor. The big removals firms just don't touch our market because the margins aren't there", says Mark Lobban. In fact, he himself is now considering expanding into broader international removals business, where profit margins are higher and prospects for growth are better than in the niche Afro-Caribbean market, which currently accounts for around 65 percent of MPS's business. Attaining membership of The National Guild of Removers and Storers will make a difference in our bid for part of the global market.

MPS Destinations plc has in the meantime opened its own 10,000 sq ft warehouse facility handling international removals to some destinations world wide including the USA, Canada, Africa and parts of Europe. The company also handles import and export storage, and consolidations for other freight companies.

With all the synergies neatly put together it is a fair assumption that the company will continue to grow and carve out for itself a well-earned place in the mainstream of its industry.

Black businesses must aim for the mass market place and among the ways of getting on board is via franchise operations. It may well be argued that this route calls for larger sums of capital, but conversely it is also open to attracting financing from the financial markets because of being less risk averse and the huge potential that fast foods, for example, offer. A case in point is that of Tony Sealy, one of Mc Donald's busiest franchise operations.

GRAMMA'S, owned by Dounne Alexander Walker, is famous for its manufacture of herbal foods. The Proprietor is among those people who value their independence and is resolute in pursuing her ambition. It is a model black company, and a good example for young business aspirants to follow. GRAMMA'S products are unique, both in quality and presentation and has on both counts carved out a well deserved niche in the market for itself.

Bread is a staple the world over and this is no exception in the black community. The way bread is made varies from town to town and country to country.

Sunrise Bakery, based in Birmingham, introduced its Caribbean formula in the first place to meet the need for bread and other pastry products. Hard dough bread is a Jamaican speciality and in some households, life is not the same without hard dough bread.

The company has made tremendous strides not only in meeting immigrant demand locally, but it now also supplies some leading supermarkets such as Tesco and Asda, some of whose customers have acquired a taste for the Jamaican staple.

Sunrise has grown significantly, providing local jobs and creating a sense of pride in the community. Errol Drummond, the driving force behind this progressive organisation, is on course to making it one of the community's most formidable businesses.

The leading role played by Hansib Publications Ltd in driving Black British Enterprise is legendary. The company's publications gave unstinted material support to emerging businesses, carrying advertising costs that ran into several thousand pounds which new businesses were unable to finance. This gigantic gesture is possibly not known and needs to be recognised, for without that initial support of free exposure, many would have remained unknown.

Hansib's services both to businesses and the community in general, started in 1971 with the West Indian Digest, followed in 1973 by a "who's who" of West Indians in Britain. Third World Impact followed in 1979 expanding in coverage, scope and content. Its eighth edition was published in 1988.

Arif Ali is Chief Executive and Chairman of the family firm, which pioneered regular Caribbean publishing in Britain. The firm's output included a collection of titles - West Indian World, West Indian Digest, Caribbean Times, Asian Digest, Asian Times, Root Magazine and African Times.

The impact on community life is many and varied. Work and training opportunities flowed from the company's operations. Many black journalists of today owe their professional livelihood to Hansib. The company's custom of recognising success played an important part in fostering black business development. Hansib has today under its belt in excess of one hundred titles and remains a major force in Caribbean business development.

OSWALD BENJAMIN is a haulage company located at 6 Northumberland Park Road in Tottenham that has always operated in the mainstream.

The company's success is rooted in the quality service it delivers to its customers over the years.

The company is greatly respected for its efficiency and meeting the terms of its contracts. With its disciplined and positive approach in meeting its customers requirements, OSWALD BENJAMIN's fleet could only continue to grow.

I have always contended that the engine for economic development and community advancement must be business led and driven. It is a prerequisite to growth in many directions.

The question is how must this be done? A good example is to be found in the person of Lawford Delroy Marks, an Afro Caribbean inventor of a patented electronics computer control system. His company, Future Generations, based in Rochester Kent, employs black and white staff. Marks' philosophy must be the message for thousands of young budding entrepreneurs.

"I do not believe in hand-outs or the dependence syndrome. Nobody owes me a living. Once you have acquired the necessary qualifications it is up to you decide your future. You can work for someone else or get into your own business,

but you must work hard, you must be disciplined and you must expect no special favours. The market is a cruel place, its not interested in any other consideration save your ability to deliver on quality and economy etc - as promised. Personally, I would help a man who tried hard and failed, but I have no pity for those who never try and who believe that the world owes them a living."

I concur with the sentiments of Mark. My own role in practising what I preach has been business and community related.

Emerging black business can hardly be discussed without touching on the role Dyke & Dryden Ltd played after more than three decades of involvement in one way or another in the business life of the community.

It is a well documented fact that the company pioneered the development of the black haircare industry in the UK which today employs thousands of people, and has been the spring board in assisting a number of ethnic people to practice and exercise a range of managerial and professional skills they gained at universities and colleges.

The company's equal opportunity policy was unique in its multiracial staff make up, and has been an example for many white owned businesses to follow, who constantly spoke to me about their good intentions - but yet failed to deliver on them.

Influencing change in this area had its problems, and tested senior management skills and beliefs. How to deal with unemployed blacks who questioned why do you employ white people when there were so many of us unemployed?

In the case of my white employees, did they feel isolated and uncomfortable being employed by a black owned business?

The short answer is no. Fairness and transparency prevailed in all of my dealings with employees leaving no cause and room for fear or doubting.

Black influence on change in society has as its first priority the pursuit of the right of equal opportunity - it must continue to build pressure groups and work steadfastly with existing ones to ensure that it happens. This course of action is obligatory on each of us. Why do we need pressure groupings? Firstly, because it is the conventional way of drawing attention to particular concerns, of creating awareness, and the way of getting action. Pressures for change which attract broad public support will always have a common thread running through them, they will seek more acceptable ways of doing things, which leads in the end to a more just and equitable society.

Social change is, however, constantly taking place in a variety of ways, invariably, through pressures on issues of the day as they arise. Currently we see an ongoing campaign for public propriety, for greater accountability - for open government, equality for women in management at board level, environmental campaign against pollution and a host of others. Permissible pressures enshrined in our freedoms are clearly the regulator that influence change in most democratic societies.

In the course of my business dealings I have found that there is insufficient understanding of the importance of responsible leadership based on equal opportunity, and in general, the importance of the wealth creation role for the black community as a whole. It is one of the key facts that Lord Scarman highlighted in his report on the Brixton riots.

As black businesses develop and grow, we must stress the importance of leadership that is equitable and fair and show by example how this will create the confidence needed in the pursuit of an inclusive society. It is not only in business that change must be the order of the day, but also across society as a whole. We need to see more of the kind of leadership demonstrated by persons like Bill Morris at T&G, Ken Livingstone as Mayor of London, and Heather Rabatts, former Chief Executive of the London Borough of Lambeth.

This book seeks to highlight some of the changes taking place - the patterns of change - the range and mix of activity as they relate to black business entry into the mainstream of the economy.

My observations show quite clearly a picture of the processes that are taking place. In the first place, black entrepreneurial flair is at an all time high. Second generation blacks are better educated than their parents were and, consequently, better able to tackle issues that their forbears would have had to succumb to in an effort to give their children a better future. Secondly, unfair treatment in employment practices have forced many people to choose self employment as a way forward in preparing to face the future. Thirdly, some professionals who have spent time in employment and learnt particular business skills have moved on for the challenge of the market place, applying their skills independently. In addition, information technology and globalisation have opened up a new world of opportunity for the ambitious.

What for me is now very exiting, and I am sure the good Lord Scarman must be delighted to see, is his vision of a Britain at peace with itself slowly evolving, which will in time hopefully hold up a model we can sell to the rest of the world.

Perhaps I might just underline some of the key areas in which participation is now positively taking place. The following examples will demonstrate my view.

Entry into the institutions that wield real power and authority are beginning to surface - in the Houses of Parliament, Local Government, the Civil Service and the Police, in the Army, Navy and Air Force, the judiciary and literally in all the professions.

Afro Caribbean businesses have had what I like to call temporary set backs, some through our own failings - the lack of support and trust - a situation unheard of in other communities. For example, a Jewish person will travel long distances just to support his community, the Asians and Cypriots will do the same. Unfortunately, that loyalty is missing in the black community in general. Competition, I believe, is healthy where it is fair, and good for keeping business people on their toes, but where we set out to destroy is quite another matter.

My own experiences are of such that mentioning one or two examples may make some people sit up to think of the harm they can unwittingly inflict on their own community's advancement.

An episode with a young woman, a supposedly close friend of one of my partners, highlights an example of a weird way of thinking. She stopped by our store in Ridley Road for a chat with her five year old son in tow. The little fellow, washed in tears, pressed his mother to buy him a toy on display, without success.

On noting the child's distress, my colleague handed him the toy as a gift. His eyes lit up, he was all smiles. His mother thanked my colleague and they went their way, only for my colleague to note that she stopped at a store selling the same merchandise as we did and purchased a product that we also sold.

The lady was quite well known to my colleague and on her way back, he challenged her about her failure to support his business and invited her to tell him whether he was uncompetitive or was it that his service not was not to her liking.

It turned out that we were in fact even cheaper on the item she bought, and only to be told that she shopped at our competitor's store purely out of habit!

Incidents like these help to explain a conflict in the minds of some members of our community, which I hope is merely a passing phase in outlook.

The scale of African-Caribbean business is by far fewer in numbers than in some of the other ethnic groups.

The Asian community for example is way out in front of all groups. In the scheme of things, some groups will always be out front, and as I have already explained. Whether by design or by accident, the black community has been dealt an unfair deal.

What is important however, and is clearly evident, is that we are not all sitting around and moaning about the past. There is currently a positive mindset to work hard and improve our place in society. A spirited and positive attitude to correct earlier failures is surfacing all the time and can be seen in the diversity and range of involvement taking place across the board.

I had already alluded to factual evidence and will now pick at random a few more businesses, some sung and unsung heroes who are taking this process forward.

Urban Ray De Freitas from Trinidad became managing director of Rossis Frozen Foods in Manor Park, East London. His compatriot, K.N. Maharaj, was director of Chris Foreign Foods (Wholesalers) Ltd, importers of tropical foods in South-East London.

Curtis Francis, a Grenadian, managed a successful export company to the Windward Islands. Barry John, a Trinidadian was among the first to establish a photographic business in the community and has operated for years at Finsbury Park, North London. Junior Lincoln combined with Rupert Cunningham to form Bamboo Records, and helped to build the community's music industry.

Trinidadian brothers - Harry and Roger Simmons - opened Magfa Motors Ltd in Clapham, South London. Harry started his working life as a motor mechanic apprentice, while Roger gained a City & Guilds certificate in motor engineering. Their combined technical competence led to a resounding success of their company.

Hugh Scotland was one of the most flamboyant and multi-faceted characters of the 1960s. He arrived in Britain from Trinidad in the 1940s, and was a qualified lawyer. In his varied career, Scottie, as he was fondly called, was the first black impresario in Europe.

Scotland challenged the colour bar in the entertainment industry and succeeded in having it lifted in many sectors. He promoted shows ranging from annual beauty contests at the Lyceum to social events at his Wisky A Go-Go Club in Soho.

Jamaican George Martin believes that West Indians should be business-minded in order to secure economic independence. He and his wife demonstrated their many enterprise skills in several successful business projects.

Their catering output is always a firm favourite wherever it is presented, leaving its customer base always coming back for more. George is by profession a talented motor mechanical engineer. He managed the Crouch Hall Garage in North London for some years before moving into his new business.

The family owns and manage a (soft furnishings) company. V J Martin & Sons is famous for its interior designs and is a favourite supplier to up-market clients.

His community interests and involvement are so numerous, that they would run into volumes.

Martin Lewis, another Jamaican, converted his mechanical expertise to a proficient radio and television engineer. He came to Britain after living for a while in the US, obtained a City & Guilds diploma and opened his own business. Lewis felt strongly that young black people should take advantage of educational opportunities that were open to them.

Delvin Ruddock, who was born in Jamaica, attended Bristol Technical College and as a mechanical engineer, became an electronics specialist. He provided a home-based service for customers with cars. He too supported the idea of more young West Indians obtaining apprenticeships in various fields.

The last 10 years has seen black enterprise development moving into areas serving the wider community. Barbadian Clyde Pile is a leading black industrialist in the city of Birmingham where he founded Glassworks Limited in the 1980s, which is today Glass Merchants Ltd. Pile's business in glass expanded during the height of the economic recession during the late 80s / early 90s. His other business interests includes a subsidiary engaged in franchising and the Birmingham Syndicate.

Another Caribbean son whose entrepreneurial gifts have blossomed in the Midlands is Aruba-born Tex Flint who has been residing in Britain for over a generation. A self-taught musician, businessman and community leader, Flint started work as a salesman with a Canadian company. In 1982 he set up his own fast food shop. A few years later, he expanded to three shops, selling two of them in order to invest in the main food chain. As a medium scale operator, he produces an exclusive range of tropical spices for various types of food.

Sheffield is well known for its soccer fever and other social events. Little is known about the commercial talent of the Caribbean community. Frederick Chattoo, who left Jamaica in the 1960s to join his parents in Britain, is making a name for himself up north. In 1983 a private company voted him 'Apprentice of the Year'. After working briefly as a manager with the Sheffield Health Authority, he bought the Alpha Hotel in 1994. Operating in a white-dominated industry was not easy for him, but his market research paid dividends. He has since refurbished the hotel, adding a restaurant to cater for both Caribbean and English cuisine. He is a member of the management committee of the African Caribbean Centre in Sheffield. He is convinced that Alpha will set a new trend in both the hotel and tourism industry.

Indeed, there is hardly a settlement in the country from the Highlands of Scotland to the Western Country in which we have not contributed to small business development and local enterprise.

This relatively small survey points positively without doubt to the direction in which the community is heading.

Rudi Page
Managing Director
Statecraft Consulting
Ltd

Joy Nichols
Managing Director
Nichols Employment Agency

Dr Ken Ife
Chairman & Chief Executive
Technology Centre

Education

Africans and West Indians have also excelled in every facet of education (including the British instructional system) since time immemorial. Since the last century, former colonies have produced international giants, especially in the academic and political spheres. The late Dr. Eric Williams was an accomplished historian before he became Prime Minister of the twin-island republic of Trinidad and Tobago. As a senior statesman of the Caribbean, he was instrumental in the establishment of the regional integration movement, starting with the Caribbean Free Trade Association (CARIFTA) and later, the Caribbean Community (CARICOM) based on the Treaty of Chaguaramas in Port-of-Spain, 1973. Few can remember that it was during his studies in Britain and the US that he produced some of his most brilliant works in education and history, including 'From Capitalism to Slavery'— and 'The history of Trinidad and Tobago'. He was actively involved in the black student movement in London. In the early 1960s, Dr. Williams was one of the architects behind the setting up of the University of the West Indies (UWI) - he believed in academic freedom in the region.

Another Caribbean genius was Guyanese scholar, politician and Pan-Africanist, Dr. Walter Rodney who before his tragic death in 1980 left his stamp on African scholarship universally. He studied at the School of Oriental and African Studies at the University of London. His writings including 'How Europe Underdeveloped Africa'— and 'The History of the Upper Guinea Coast'— and his strong Pan-Africanist ideals, are still relevant today as they were decades ago. While sections of European academia have distorted much of his work, Rodney's enormous contribution to black scholarship and universal enlightenment is irrefutable. The Caribbean community - at home and abroad - have immortalised both Williams and Rodney by naming organisations and institutions after them.

Colonial education in the Caribbean was one of rigidity and imposition. While white missionaries applied religion as a code of conformity, Caribbean people used Christian values to achieve excellence in various branches of the natural and social sciences. What we need is to fuse our resources to create more opportunities for succeeding generations in the Caribbean and those who are abroad. Thus the painstaking documentation of the labours of previous and succeeding generations is an essential step towards our ultimate success in enterprise culture.

From academics of a more contemporary age, Dr. Harry Goulbourne was born in Jamaica and was educated at the Peckham Manor Comprehensive School, South London. He obtained his doctorate at the University of Sussex after reading history and political theory at the University of Lancaster. Dr. Goulbourne lectured in Tanzania and then was appointed Vice-Dean of the Faculty of Social Sciences at the UWI, Mona Campus, Jamaica. He was awarded a Leverhulme Fellowship at the Centre for Caribbean Studies at Warwick where he became a Senior Research Fellow. His books include 'Politics and State in the Third World'. He is a member of the Caribbean Studies Association, the Association of African Political Scientists and Gray's Inn.

Vincentian Dr. Philip Nanton read business studies at Hendon College of Technology. After achieving a post-graduate diploma in economic development (with distinction) at the University of London, he obtained a Masters degree in Economics and African Studies at the University of Birmingham and read for his doctorate at the University of Sussex. From there he returned to the University of Birmingham as lecturer in social policy. Dr. Nanton's published works comprise the 'Melanthika anthology' and 'Anancy's Magic'.

Majorie Saunders provides a good example of the connection between teaching and religion. She was born in Jamaica and lived in Canada before coming to the United Kingdom. She holds a certificate of proficiency in religious knowledge from the University of London. She is author of the booklet, 'Living in Britain'. She was president of the Sheffield and District West Indian Association, the Business and Professional Women's Club, the British Caribbean Association and the Sheffield Council for Community Relations, as well as a member of school management and government boards. A deaconess in the United Reform Church, Saunders attended missionary college in Edinburgh, Scotland.

Clarence Eugene Lindsday from St. Vincent arrived in Britain after residing in the US where he studied at Boston and Tufts Universities respectively. He was founder and secretary of the International Caribbean Association and executive member of the Hackney Community Relations Council. Lindsday played the violin in the Haringey Symphony Orchestra and was appointed head of education at the Edith Cavell School. He listed walking and music as his hobbies after completing his professional and social work.

Specialist teachers moved later into various branches of the community relations industry and into local government administration. Pauline Abbott-

Butler holds a Bachelor of Education degree and was a nurse and teacher before becoming president of the African Caribbean Educational Project and National Council for St. Vincent and the Grenadines Women (UK). Betty Campbell was appointed headmistress of the Mount Stewart Primary School. She was born in Cardiff, trained as a teacher and achieved an Honours degree in education. Later, Ms. Campbell obtained a Masters degree in multicultural curriculum.

Two primary examples of specialist schools of distinction - which are now blazing the education trail, and producing extraordinary results in the process, are profiled in this section

Ghanaian Osei Asibey Kwateng, a Business Educationalist, is the name and driving force behind the CITY OF LONDON BUSINESS COLLEGE.

Touched in 1990 by the plight of black ethnic minority youth and their under achievement, he was convinced that this was to a large extent down to their poor basic educational qualification, and was moved to do something about it. Out of this passionate concern came the founding of New Era College.

Osei Kwateng understood only too well that good employment opportunities and the ability to compete in the market place depended on being equipped to do so. The advent of New Era College was gratefully received fulfilling a gap needing encouragement and support at the grass roots in what was, and still is, one of the most depressed London inner city areas.

The College's ground-breaking emergence provided practical training in various business oriented courses which were meant to prepare and empower young people enough to face the many challenges loaded against them. In 1995 the name of the college was changed to City of London Business College that more reflects the strong business orientation of the of the institution. On 27th August 1996 the new name received certified incorporation.

The organisation's aims and objectives were clearly stated and rigorously followed. (1) to bridge the gap between those who had only the basic educational qualification and those without GCSE and A levels and thus virtually no chance to higher education. (2) Encourage as many people of diverse talents and backgrounds as possible to explore and enhance their abilities and capabilities in Business Education. (3) To offer formal education to academically orientated individuals who wish to develop and prepare themselves well for much higher education. (4) To create additional conducive educational conditions in the Haringey community to raise the living standards of the people of this multi-cultural and impoverished Borough.

Highlighting the track record of this committed institution in doing its level best to improve the black community's position in the field of education is central to our place in this society. The significance of the College's mission cannot be taken lightly, representing as it does the cornerstone, the foundation and fabric of a learning community. Getting the college off the ground was a Herculean task, one which encountered problems from which men of lesser vision and stamina would have run away. Not so for Osei Kwateng, he is a leader with a burning desire to improve the lot of the black community and is characterised by the many roadblocks that he encountered and pushed aside in getting where the college is today. He is deservedly a very proud Principal.

The institution's scholarly achievement by which it is judged is substantive with many of its students obtaining top grades of Merit and Distinction. Three outstanding students were of world class obtaining gold medals. They were Wellington Guchu for arithmetic in 1999, Mr. A. H. English for Business Communication Skills 2001 and Mr. Opoku Kwofie, for Arithmetic in 2001. This solid achievement is against a background of battles that had to be fought with a reluctant Council's Planning Department, and the unhelpful bank support.

City of London Business College takes pride in hosting notable black events. A good example is last October's most inspiring international symposium titled," Engaging Learning with Entrepreneurship & culture" which brought speakers from various parts of the world. Celebrating Black History month in November 2002 was another great occasion highlighting, whilst keeping alive, the consciousness of the black contribution at the national and international levels.

Osei Kwateng's philosophy speaks to us all loud and clear, *"unless we do what has to be done for ourselves, no one will do it for us"*.

Caribbean professionals are today market leaders in education, an important sector which is often taken for granted, although it generates millions for the economy and also sustains Britain's knowledge industry. One leading institution is TCS Tutorial College, the first of its kind in Britain and Europe, founded by the extraordinary Caribbean educator and literature specialist, Dr Roselle Antoine, who is also Principal of the institution

Beginning as a Language School in 1994 to cater for foreign students, TCS grew into a multi-disciplinary and inter-departmental education and training institution   During its early stages of development, Dr. Antoine soon saw the need to service the local community due to demands for Supplementary education, and four years later, The TCS Supplementary School was born. This attracted students from ethnic minority communities, changing the face of the student population to a mini United Nations. With its infectious motto, "I am somebody Great", the curriculum included core subjects such as English, Maths, French, Science, IT and Caribbean Studies.

This area of the organization excelled in demonstrating that it was second to none, evidenced by its Accreditation to the University of Cambridge for the delivery of Key English and Preliminary English tests, Cambridge University Young Enterprise Centre, OCR (Oxford, Cambridge and Royal Society of Arts) exams at GCSE level and AQA (Assessment and Qualifications Authority), GCSE, GNVQ, NVQ, IT, A Level and many professional Information Technology courses and a Cambridge University Young Learners Centre.

Dr Antoine insists that accessing the curriculum from a multi-disciplinary standpoint is sometimes necessary to include those without purely academic qualifications, and like an astute business woman and educator, expanded the organizations departments to include TCS Centre for Caribbean Studies, a Caribbean Dramatic Society, and a Black Writers Group, in order to harness an inter-generational captive community.

This offered education to both academically orientated and talented, skilled individuals who are able to prepare for Further and Higher education as well as Life Skills training.

Not only is the developmental vision of the institution located within the walls of the organization, but Dr Antoine has demonstrated that achievement must be seen as an ongoing goal to strive for and in 1999 she began what is now popularly known as *"The Principal's Community Achievement Awards"*, an action which continually links the children's achievement with that of the community in an effort to show that achievement is ongoing. During the past 5 years, TCS has awarded at least 8 outstanding community members for over 10 years of tireless commitment to the Black community.

The impetus to encapsulate the local, national with the international sense of development and achievement within the organization, was documented in July 2002 when TCS hosted the first international conference to look at the fifty years of sustainable progress in the Caribbean Contribution to the British Commonwealth - as part of the Queen's Golden Jubilee celebrations. This helped to authenticate the impact Caribbean peoples have made to Britain and the wider Commonwealth, with delegates from the USA (Professor Kamau Brathwaite), University of the West Indies (Professor Gordon Rohlchr), University of East London (Dr Kimani

Nehusi), Mrs. Patsy Robertson, Director of Information from the Commonwealth Secretariat, together with a compliment of Caribbean High Commissioners, academics from community development, social inclusion, business and education arenas.

TCS Tutorial College's brief is expansive, taking the essence of its motto, *"I am Somebody Great,"* very seriously indeed. Dr Antoine has concluded that the value of role modeling cannot be minimized. TCS had set out to lead the way in providing information which synthesizes the history of excellent pioneers and the need to revisit the paths of progress which are, in effect, role models in our time hitherto inaccessible to our youths. To remedy this, TCS has a Publication Department, which has produced a Caribbean Greats Series. This provides booklets as well as Memorial Lectures on Caribbean Leaders as an active and creative learning approach. Again, this has grown into an international participatory activity, culminating the recent International Marryshow Day 2002, last year.

Unlike other education institutions, TCS is not a recipient of statutory funding - it is self-financing. It has however developed constructive partnerships with local authorities and other public agencies in delivering education as well as spearheading economic research beneficial to the local community.

In advancing a viable solution to underachievement, Dr Antoine has advocated a TCS Model of Excellence, which includes Caribbean Orature as a requisite tool for creative education and business. By fusing strands of cultural histories with artistic elements, owners of businesses and social enterprises in the Caribbean community can increase their competitive advantage. Dr. Antoine is convinced that such a model will result equally in the alleviation of the current skills gap affecting Britain.

TCS Principal's role is no mean feat and this has been continuously recognized over the past 5 years. Dr Roselle Antoine has an impressive list of literary achievements. In 1981 she won the Young Black Writers Award for her essay "Blackness is a Source of Strength", and has since then written children's stories, a play and continues to research in the Development of Orature and its impact on Anglo-Caribbean Writings.

In l999 the High Commissioner for Grenada, Carriacou and Petite Martinique, awarded her a Certificate of Appreciation, for 'Outstanding Contribution to Multiculturalism and Education'. In 2001 the Supplementary Schools Support Service (A Department for Education initiative) awarded her with a Certificate of Achievement 2001 for *"working tirelessly for 18 years to help thousands of children in difficulty and enable them to achieve their true potential"*. During that same year, Dr Antoine was elected a Fellow of the Royal Society for the Arts for her work and her contribution to business, education and commerce.

In 2002 the London and Thames Today newspaper presented the College with the Business Achievement Award for Education Excellence and the Journal Publishing Company awarded its *"Award of Merit"* for Education Services in 2002. The work and ethos of TCS College is synonymous with Dr Antoine, and this was clearly recognized by a most prestigious award presented to Dr. Antoine as Businesswoman of the Year January 2003.

Dr Antoine is committed to education excellence in all forms of human endeavour. She advocates independence as a tool for self-development, and over the last two years has created The Roselle Antoine Foundation, a registered charity, set up to advance education and in particular special education needs, especially those who are underachieving or at risk of exclusion from education in general.

The Charity's vision, like the vision of TCS Tutorial College, encapsulates the vision of its leader; that in order to reach our true potential, we must provide strategies to deal with problems among our communities, in encouraging responsibility for learning; goal-setting and good citizenship; working in conjunction with a variety of agencies and institutions to find practical solutions; mobilizing resources for viable programs to support children, and promoting forms of education that enable young people to engage positively with the growing complexity and diversity of social values and ways of life.

Dr. Antoine believes in practicing what you preach and her latest expansion to the TCS Education Network is the TCS Independent School, with its goal to provide the community with an alternative institution, committed to educational excellence and leadership.

Jocelyn Barrow was awarded the order of the British Empire (OBE) in 1972 and became a Dame in 1992, for her services to the community and her contribution to education. She graduated from the University of London with a degree in English. She held positions, including vice-president of the Townswomen's Guild, a governor of the British Broadcasting Corporation and chair of the East London Housing Association. She married Jamaican Henderson Downer, a barrister of Lincoln's Inn and the Jamaican Bar.

Trevor Carter is a member of the National Union of Teachers and was employed as an educational adviser by the Inner London Education Authority (ILEA). Born in Trinidad, he has been a member of the executive committee of WISC and chaired the board of directors of the Black Theatre Co-op. Dr. Michael Gilkes, a senior lecturer in English at the UWI (Cave Hill Campus, Barbados), was awarded a Lever Hulme Fellowship in Caribbean Studies by the University of Warwick. He obtained his doctorate from the University of Kent and his books on Caribbean literature include 'The West Indian Novel'. As a literary giant in modern Caribbean literature, he is the driving force behind the documentation of oral traditions and other popular art forms. He has written and edited several anthologies. In the early 1990s, he shook the European intellectual community when he challenged the perpetual myth of Christopher Columbus' discovery of the West Indies during his voyages in the 15th century.

Councillor Eddie Griffith is one of several teachers to be elected to local government office. He was born in Barbados and holds a Bachelor of Science degree and a teaching certificate. Griffith was a member of the National Union of Teachers, the British Caribbean Association and the Newham African Caribbean Association, chair of the governing body of Highgate Wood Secondary School and Head of Politics and Social Education at a London school. He has a keen interest in youth affairs.

Councillor Joseph 'Joe' Abrams, a former Mayor of Merton, obtained a Bachelor of Arts degree at the University of London. He was head of pastoral care at Bow Boys School, East London, where he chaired the National Association of Community Relations Councils.

Donald Hinds had a varied career - being a bus conductor and a writer of short stories and articles. He obtained a Master of Arts degree and headed the history department at Geoffrey Chaucer School. Music teacher and organist, Anthony Carl Jackson, was educated at the Royal Academy of Music, Downing College, Cambridge and the University of London. He is a member of the Incorporated Society of Musicians and a Fellow of the Royal College of Organists. He teaches at the Whitgift School in Croydon and plays the organ at Croydon Parish Church.

Ms. Wanjiru Kihoro studied at Columbia University in New York and completed an MA in Development Studies at Leeds University. She became the education and programme officer at the Africa Centre in London. Her interests covered film, drama, writing, reading, and singing. Councillor Ken Layne, born in Barbados, has specialised in educational matters. He is an executive member of the National Anti-racist Movement in Education and is also a school governor. He is education officer for the National Communications Union and served on the London Borough of Haringey's education committee.

Councillor Lloyd King, a Jamaican, qualified as an electrician and later gained an honours degree in education at the Polytechnic of North London (now the University of North London). He is a member of the National Association of Local Government Officers and is a founder member of the Hackney Education and Development Society. In addition to helping black children to cope with the difficulties associated with education, Cllr King was involved in projects to help the black elderly. He once chaired Hackney Council for Racial Equality and has campaigned for better library facilities. His main concerns are the establishment of equal opportunities in housing, education and social services.

Zimbabwean-born Jim Mthethwa is a teacher. He represented his borough on the ILEA. He has a BA (Sociology) and an MA (Government Politics), City of London Polytechnic. Mthethwa is an authorised member for Rural and Urban (Education) Centres and for Community and Voluntary Initiatives within the London area. Guyanese Russell Profit was educated at Goldsmiths College, University of London. After an early career in teaching, he became Principal Race Advisor with the London Borough of Brent. He is a prominent political activist.

Trinidadian-born Lee Ramdeen obtained a Master of Education degree at Digby College in London. She was appointed successively director of the ILEA's Primary Development Project for pupils of Caribbean origin and Inspector of Multi-ethnic Education. She became Assistant Chief Education Officer in the London Borough of Haringey and has chaired Cardinal Basil Humes Committee for the Caribbean Community.

Former international off-spinner, Reggie Scarlett, is a staff coach with the National Cricket Association, cricket consultant with the London Community Cricket Association and chief coach at Haringey Cricket College. He has contributed to various publications on cricket and related sporting activities in Britain and the Caribbean.

Jamaican Elaine Sihera, could qualify for mention in several chapters. She gained a BA (Sociology and Education) from the Open University and a post-graduate certificate in education from Cambridge University. She is a member of Women in Management and the Institute of Journalists and was formerly an information officer with the Royal Air Force at Brize Norton and an English teacher. She edited 'Impact', a magazine aimed at publicising (among other things) the contribution of the Ethnic Minority enterprise culture and its impact on equal opportunities policy. She is also head of a training consultancy called ESP, which won two Department of

Employment awards.

Baroness Scotland is also a classic professional gem, becoming the first Black female Queen's Counsel in 1991 at the age of 35. In 1976, she graduated with a law degree and joined the Middle Temple one year later. Quiet and unassuming, little is known about her political convictions, but yet her achievements in legal education and community development are admired and envied alike. She is currently a Minister in the Labour Government.

The late Brian Sullivan was Assistant Director of the Polytechnic of North London. He was born in Cardiff, and obtained a degree in Economics at Hull University. After a spell with the RAF, he studied at the University of London, earning an MSc. After spending two years lecturing in Nigeria, he was appointed senior lecturer at Huddersfield University. Three years on, he headed a department at Ealing College of Higher Education and represented the North London Branch of Full-employ. Brian was a truly rounded academic.

Councillor Bernard Wiltshire was elected Deputy Leader of the ILEA. He was born in Dominica and is a barrister and lecturer with particular experience in education. Cllr Wiltshire taught at universities in New York, Jamaica, Dominica, and chaired the governors of Hackney College, and the Black Governors Collective. He pioneered the first supplementary school in the borough and conducted research into the achievement of black pupils at Hackney Downs School.

Another African Caribbean son, whose consistency and dedication to both education and law earned him and his community great respect, is Guyanese-born Sir Herman Ouseley, (now Lord Ouseley). In 1993 he was elected the first black chair of the national Commission for Racial Equality (CRE). Five years earlier, in March 1988, he was appointed Chief Executive of the ILEA after serving as Director of Education in the authority. Previously, he held senior positions in a distinguished public service career. He was a member of the inquiry into the disturbances in Birmingham - Handsworth in 1985, and was formerly Principal Race Adviser and Head of the Ethnic Minorities Unit of the then Greater London Council (GLC). Outside his main profession, he chaired the voluntary Ujima Housing Association and has been committee member on the editorial Advisory Board for the Equal Opportunities Review and for the Institute of Race Relations. While Lord Ouseley has been criticised by some for his so-called luke-warm response to controversial issues in the black community, his persistent advocacy on a stable race relations climate in Britain cannot be disputed.

Councillor Les Francis was born in Jamaica and has lived in Britain for more than thirty years. He is a multi-faceted professional - a teacher, former engineer, welder, railway-worker, bus conductor, and more recently, a driver-attendant for Greenwich Social Services. His commitment to education is evidenced by his governorship of ILEA schools and colleges, coupled with his desire to defend budgetary cuts in education. Francis is actively involved in community initiatives, including youth projects, Age Concern and his borough's employment resource unit.

The findings of the 2001 Census figures confirms without any doubt the direction in which the Black education performance is heading.

I quote the Times headline of 8th May 2003 "Black Africans in Britain lead way in education". The article continues. "Black and Asian people born in Britain make up half the country's non-white population, for the first time according to results from the 2001 census.

The published figures show that members of many ethnic minority groups are better educated and more likely to hold professional jobs than British white people; and they are more likely to be in good health.

Commentators said the findings, which cover England and Wales, marked a significant milestone in Britain's cultural history.

Principal Osei Kwateng
City of London Business College

Press & Publications

The African Caribbean community needed its own newspaper. From the earliest days, we got news from the mainstream radio, television and Fleet Street. Yet we wanted to have our own media to provide a sense of identity, harmony and purpose, while advertising community events, services and businesses. Publishing indeed was one of the first enterprises attempted and has been the most difficult to sustain.

The West Indian Gazette, published by Claudia Jones from South London in the late 1950s, was the first real attempt to publish a regular newspaper for the black community. Although it was very much radical and left wing, it reflected the hopes and aspirations of its readers. Through its coverage of national and international issues, it was an alternative to the mainstream press. Such encouragement was necessary, especially in the aftermath of the Notting Hill riots.

As with most campaigning publications, the Gazette demonstrated journalistic zeal and enthusiasm rather than efficient management. Circulation was affected by a lack of advertising, promotion and marketing skills and as a consequence, the publication became irregular and eventually ceased entirely on Claudia's premature death in the early 1960s. It should be said that the Trinidadian's entry into journalism was as a direct result of her civil rights campaign, particularly against the unjust Jim Crow laws in the US. On her release from prison there, she came to Britain to continue her universal struggle against race discrimination. The West Indian Gazette, therefore, was an ideal platform to give her campaign effect.

However, the first recorded Black publications in Britain were those edited by Celestine Edwards during the 1880s. The journal 'Lux' appeared around 1893 and a monthly magazine, 'Fraternity', was first published in Liverpool in July 1893.

At the end of the war, the Black Press developed in Britain. In 1952 Caribbean News first appeared, published by the London Branch of the Caribbean Labour Congress. It sought to be a people's paper. It existed between 1952 and 1956. The West Indian Gazette was launched in 1958 and it became the concrete expression of the dreams of many black people in Britain.

About the same time, Flamingo was published as a glossy, professional, informative monthly magazine. It was owned by Europeans, but was staffed exclusively by African Caribbean personnel. The magazine provided articles on black heritage, news in Britain and abroad, glamour, and human interest, all of which were supplemented by photographs. Flamingo's historical culture and investigative-style journalism was unequalled by its successors.

Although it lasted between two and three years, Flamingo's influence was profound. Space was allocated to established writers and towards developing younger talent. Syd Burke, better known today as a radio broadcaster, was the photographic element of the pen-picture partnership with Eric McAlpine. Bill Patterson, himself a prominent photographer, was also a contributor.

Aubrey Baynes took up the baton which Claudia Jones left. His strength too, was in journalism and commitment rather than in business efficiency. Baynes was in no way less resolute in his political and social opinions. However, his publications such as Daylight, had a more racy layout content, with a higher profile on entertainment and sport. He was in the right position to take advantage of the first serious attempt to launch an African Caribbean weekly newspaper.

For the brief period of their existence, Baynes was editor of Magnet News and Cinnamon in the mid-1960s. The high quality contributors included: Jan Carew, who was the editor for the initial edition of Magnet News, classical music conductor, Rudolph Dunbar, Andrew Salkey, Ernest Eytle, Barbara Blake - who later became a Jamaican senator - and fashion writer, Sheila Brown, who would realise the dream of black weekly press.

Baynes learnt the lessons of business failure and personality rivalries which undermined Magnet News and Cinnamon. Preparation for his next journalistic endeavour took at least four years. By 1970, he was in a position to launch the West Indian World in spite of considerable financial and professional difficulties. While it achieved its broad objectives, the World did not appear on time weekly.

During this critical period, Aubrey performed the duties of editor and publisher. This gave him the opportunity to draw on specialist skills and develop new talent without any threat to his own position from within the organisation. His great pioneering and leadership efforts in the industry, however, were short-lived. This time insufficient advertising and his proven business weakness bedevilled him.

In 1973, Baynes handed over the World to Guyanese Arif Ali who was then the publisher of the smaller monthly magazine - West Indian Digest.

Ali exhibited business flair and an unsurpassed grasp of public relations, which changed the newspaper from an organ of local news into a publication of international proportion. This approach brought Ali universal respect and enhanced his own reputation in the black community.

However, the publication's reputation was destroyed by several internal conflicts over the next decade. Ali was unseated by an office coup in 1976 and his successor, Russell Pierre, suffered the same fate. By the beginning of the 1980s, control had passed to Caudley George and Tony Douglas, who had joined the staff as apprentices under Baynes, but when they fell out, the closure of the newspaper was inevitable.

At that time it seemed that the work of the pioneers had been in vain. The World was in decline and the only comparable publication was the weekly Gleaner, whose position was significantly different. It was the overseas edition of an established newspaper in Jamaica and not a newspaper produced in Britain. Perhaps, it is appropriate to examine the multiple difficulties, which beset the industry.

Advertising itself was not a problem, but inadequate sponsorship had a negative effect on production costs. While major advertisers showed disinterest in meagre circulation, local businesses were reluctant to provide substantial investment in this direction. Publishers of black newspapers and other publications therefore, had to turn to local government and public agencies for sponsorship. As a temporary measure, they also sought injection of capital from influential sources, including the hair and beauty trade. The latter in effect bank-rolled, if not sustained for a little while, the West Indian World.

Writers who were attracted to a black press had strong political beliefs and needed an appropriate channel, which they could not find anywhere else to express such feelings. However, the moment a particular view was published, it offended and turned away those of a different persuasion. Fleet Street has newspapers ranging in opinions from the Morning Star to the Daily Mail. The one or other African Caribbean newspaper in itself had to encompass reporting on the gamut of political and social issues or risk losing potential support.

There is another problem which the national mainstream newspapers do not have to consider. On the one hand, the older generation of early immigrants and their children, who have a sense of regional identity, want to read news about their homelands, which are ignored otherwise. On the other hand, the younger people are more interested in what is happening among their peers in Britain and the issues, which directly affect them. No matter how hard the editor tries to achieve balance, he/she is sure to neglect a section of the media audience.

In its declining years, the West Indian World in particular, failed to maintain a balance between the serious and the frivolous in its editorial content. Once again, the national press had the luxury of choice, through its broad range of tabloids - like the Sun, and the broadsheets including the Financial Times - unlike African Caribbean newspapers. Somehow one publisher had to stamp his image on the industry, but it wasn't easy.

Generally speaking, newspapers serving the black community have a tendency, to date, to be biased towards a radical left-wing political agenda. This is not surprising since their main objective in the first place is to kick against the status quo. Such a bold approach however, stifled the black press, causing most publications to be cut off from major instruments of support, finance, advertising and general patronage.

At one level there had to be investigations into day-to-day social affairs, including the relationship between our young people and the police, racial discrimination in employment, and the problems of inner-city housing and education. At the other spectrum, their readers expected newspapers to comment on apartheid in South Africa and the politics of the so-called Third World. It was almost certain that these two distinct positions would become either blurred or confused.

At the time he took over from Aubrey Baynes at the West Indian World, Ali was a comparatively minor figure in the community's publishing. His West Indian Digest was little more than an irregularly produced handbook. Yet in that same year, he had shown his vision and his understanding of publicity, by producing the first Who's Who of West Indians in Britain, with an official launch at a dinner in the Hilton Hotel.

The Guyanese had two extraordinary qualities, which made him distinctly different from both his predecessors and would-be successors. From an early stage of his publishing endeavours, he understood the vagaries of the newspaper publishing industry and their impact on the black community. He was a workaholic and was proud to do any task to fulfil his vision. Those who were highly critical of his methods he employed in the family-owned Hansib Publishing Company in north London were forced to admit that against the backdrop of constant pressures on the black press in Britain, Ali rode the tide as an effective tactician and strategist.

The early West Indian Digest resembled a primitive Reader's Digest, on which it was based. It carried information for its specialist readership. The first editions contained a number of 'fillers' to make up the pages. Yet this publication set a precedent that was distinctive in character prior to other publications. This gave the magazine even greater impetus when the publisher's fortunes took a turn for the better at the end of the decade.

Ali made an immediate impact at the West Indian World. He projected an international image, being pictured with world leaders and other prominent personalities. His critics complained about his development of a personality cult, but be that as it may, his activities raised the newspaper's profile from being simply a local newspaper to that of an international medium of information and communication.

Soon he suffered a double setback. In his absence, his staff removed him from office, while his attempt to produce a rival, West Indian Voice, proved unsuccessful. By 1980 however, the determined Ali was back in business. This time he set about building a publishing empire that was rare in its conception and scale in the black community in Britain.

Although the West Indian Digest was revived as a more professional production, achieving a high standard of journalistic excellence, the now weekly Caribbean Times was the flagship of Hansib Publishing. CT campaigned on a range of issues of interest to the African Caribbean community, nationally and internationally. The articles were generally informative, enlightened and authoritative and the newspaper attracted established editors, columnists, journalists and young enthusiastic press personnel.

Very quickly, the publishing house expanded to incorporate African and Asian Times, along with the corresponding Digest editions. Each advance was marked by an equal acquisition of equipment and an increase in staff. The company provided an encouraging contrast to the early one-man enterprises in which publishers and aides did everything similar to how the West Indian Digest itself started.

Since Hansib Publishing gained pre-eminence in black publishing, the Voice founded in 1982 (along with its features-based sister publication-The Journal), and more recently the New Nation, which was established in 1996, are the only other weeklies that have been launched successfully. Although all three newspapers are funded and managed differently, there is some rivalry. The latter two have adopted a similar stance to the Caribbean Times on issues affecting the black community. Newspapers, which have taken a different view have either ceased publication, or have been forced to reduce their operations considerably. In early 1997, Ali announced the sale of Hansib's newspaper production line. He said that his company wanted to concentrate more on full-time publishing. The company already has over 100 titles to its credit - including books on cricket, education, history, literature and politics. Hansib is today the largest black publishing company in the UK.

The Voice today is distinctly Britain's leading newspaper founded in 1982 by the late Val Mc Calla. It is well designed with a simple layout and a runaway success, appealing to the young with the right balance of reading material for its market segment.

Root, published originally by Godfrey Hope, was the only monthly magazine that addressed specific issues on entertainment and fashion. It came into existence on the wave of Nigerian investment following that country's oil boom in the late 1970s, and described itself as being the publication for black achievers. Root, too, is a recent addition to Hansib Publications. Chic also became stabilised as an expression of beauty, fashion and related interests to the younger generation.

The introduction of regional and local radio stations opened new avenues for the promotion of music, news and general entertainment. Therefore, it complemented the print media in its decision to maintain quality news coverage in its editorial content. Steve Bernard and Greg Edwards were among the first radio comperes to acquire celebrity status for their performance in general broadcasting - both as newscasters and music moderators.

Not all radio is frivolous or light-hearted. Syd Burke's programmes for the London Broadcasting Company - Rice 'n' Peas and latterly, Tell Syd - concentrated on news stories with an earnest community and cultural appeal. Their programmes included items on visits to Britain by distinguished personalities from the Caribbean. While these programmes were restricted to Sundays, Black Londoners on Radio London had the greatest scope for broadcasting each weekday evening.

Alex Pascall, an erstwhile singer, folk raconteur and communicator, became the voice associated most closely with Black Londoners. Since the middle of the 1980s, other announcers shared the programme. There is hardly an important event or visit which the programme did not cover. Tony Williams however, is probably the best known radio disc jockey of reggae music.

Naturally, television newscasters and reporters have a high profile. Sir

Trevor McDonald and Moira Stuart are today institutional media celebrities in their own way. McDonald is the leading television anchorman in Britain, especially on the News At Ten programme. For nearly two decades, the Trinidadian-born Mc Donald has been an icon of the British media industry, especially in television. For the last five or so years, he has been crowned top newscaster/presenter. In early July 1997, he produced a remarkable programme to celebrate the British hand-over of Hong Kong to the China. The programme reflected a classic example of objective reporting, interviewing and remarkable commentary.

McDonald, now Sir Trevor, worked his apprenticeship at Radio Trinidad before transferring to the BBC World Service and thence to television. He was the first journalist to interview Nelson Mandela after his release in 1990 and the first to get an interview with Saddam Hussein, as the Gulf war loomed ahead. He is known for his common sense, curiosity, humour and persistence.

But there are other young brooding talents in the British media. Clive Myrie is described as BBC television's 'hottest foreign correspondent'. He is said to have turned down lucrative contracts from Cable News Network (CNN) in the US and other media institutions.

The jazz lover and journalist was born in Bolton to a Jamaican teacher/seamstress and a car factory foreman. After reading law at Sussex University, he was determined to be a journalist, having being motivated by McDonald in the 1970s. Myrie and Wesley Kerr are the only two black BBC network correspondents. Myrie is of the view that people who 'persevere, have talent, self-belief and are intelligent' can penetrate the corporation

As a modern media enterprise, Black Coral Productions has been prolific in nurturing and developing new talent since 1987. The business was created by Lazell Daley, a BBC-TV Producer/director with a 20-year track record, producing documentary programmes such as 'Careering Ahead', 'Help Your Child With Science', 'We are the Elephant' and 'Women Mean Business'.

Black Coral created Script City which was the first round of 'Arts For Everyone Scheme', supported by the Arts Council of England. The initiative was devised to reach a new generation of Black and Asian writers and to provide training and access into the development infrastructure of the film and TV industry for writers, script writers, editors, researchers and producers. Script City received partnership funding and professional support from British Screen, BBC and Channel 4, and forged new collaboration with other funding partners such as DNA films.

The media enterprise has produced two short films: 'Phil's Job', directed by Barnaby Southcombe and 'Killing Time', directed by Chris Beckles - both of which were on display at the 2001 Cannes Film Festival. The company is currently developing a variety of documentaries and are interested in television proposals geared towards the UK and European broadcasters.

In addition, Moira Stewart and Paul Green are among the few local and national black news presenters who are consistent with the idea of utilising their talent in the best interest of their community. Occasionally, both have been invited to officiate at high-profile social events. Regarded as a fitting role model for aspiring female entrepreneurs, Stewart in particular, participates in national and international business and media conferences and seminar/workshops.

Ebony and Black on Black have been the main specialist programmes dealing with the African Caribbean. Vince Herbert, Juliet Alexander, Beverley Anderson, and before them, Vera Gilbert, were temporary household names. But with budget restrictions and reconstruction - Ebony moved to Bristol and then under producer Vastiana Belfon, to Birmingham. This arrested the further development of such programmes from national viewing.

Since Channel Four was introduced, there has been a change of emphasis. The Bandung File, directed by Tariq Ali and Darcus Howe, was commended by the industry for its professionalism, presentation and treatment of subjects. In one hour, it examined world affairs and other issues of national interest, rather than trying to cover many topics in such limited time. In a rather refreshing initiative in 1996, Patrick Younge, a television producer produced the Black Britain series, which depicted culture, entertainment and highlights of social issues affecting the black community in Britain. A later series included clips from Africa and the Caribbean. Critics have charged that the programme should reflect a more balanced view of the black community in Britain - both the old and the young. The A Force, which was commissioned in the same year, again concentrates on pure entertainment and snippets of imitation from national television programmes such as Question Time and Blind Date programmes. With growing opportunities in the media for black programming, our producers, actors and writers, must all guard against over-simplifying characters and issues when highlighting diverse views of the African Caribbean community.

Race Today, edited by poet Linton Kwesi Johnson, occupies a similar position in the written medium. Its editorial comprises poetry, reviews, commentaries and literary compositions - all from a left-wing standpoint - from established writers. The contributors include Cyril Lionel R. James, the distinguished cricket writer, historian and Marxist commentator. In the 1930s, he wrote for the Manchester Guardian and was a close friend and associate of the famous cricketer, Sir Learie Constantine.

Pirate Radio took over from newspapers the function of publishing dances and social events, as well as propagating music. These stations have an important role in keeping the community informed, although they are not strictly legal. They are in fact transient, rarely lasting for more than a few months. To name any specific station or their operators, announcers and disc jockeys is unnecessary. Suffice to say, we do need consistently well-sponsored programmes - of news, entertainment and other issues - on both television and radio that appeal more to our community. Choice FM, although long in coming, is now a major player in serving the black community. More about the company is to be found elsewhere in this book.

Today a reader can walk into a bookshop and choose from a list of community publications: whether Caribbean, Africa and Asian Times, the Voice, the New Nation, the Gleaner, Root, Chic and other associated titles, including those from Africa and the US. The listener in turn, can tune in for news and music from conventional and sporadic radio stations. It is far removed since the older generation waited with patient expectation for the occasional issue of the West Indian Gazette.

BTV (Black Variety Television) is Britain's fastest growing television station. Michael Mowatt, Managing/Programming Director and Claudette/Producer, are the driving force behind this pioneering media network.

Its programming goes via the cable networks and the station has become one of the main outlets of regional transmission in Britain, opening doors for wider and more diverse productions. BVTV is the first cable production company to meet the needs and aspirations of the black and other ethnic minority groups, reaching a potential audience in excess of 1 million homes.

The strategic importance of the station is enormous for the black community in a number of ways. In the first place, it complements what already exists, a vibrant press and radio completing the black community media circle. Television has increasingly become the ultimate for instant news and information as it happens around the globe, it is the ultimate advertising vehicle for businesses that can afford it, and is the constant companion in every living room.

BTV is looked upon as an integral part of the world of broadcasting reaching targeted audiences positively in a way that only it can at this moment of time. Its professionalism is well respected, attracting support across the board fuelling its growth. Tune in and enjoy the very best in black programming.

We need to continue building on the efforts of those before us. Despite setbacks, they approached their tasks with immense commitment, dedication, hardwork and sacrifice. They led the way. The new generation of men and women, some of whom are making serious inroads in the ethnic and mainstream media industry, must not substitute a sense of professional pride with naked commercialism. It is important that we strive to document more of our history. We have contributed much to universal enlightenment - through ideas, often presented in essays, dissertations and theses at universities, conferences and seminars/workshops. In the words of the black Dutch Professor, Dr. Petronella Breinburg: -

"We must write our own books, publish our own newspapers, produce our own programmes for radio and television, as well as manage our own business and industry. Only through this direct method, can we be accorded with the respect and recognition we richly deserve."

The Emerging Community

Prior to their arrival in the United Kingdom, African and Caribbean people had a tradition of self-help, enterprise and an innate survival instinct. Before 1948, no laws were in place to prevent immigrants entering Britain, nor indeed the concept of British nationality. During colonial rule, the British Empire governed Africa, Asia and the Caribbean, although there were pockets of American and other European colonies known as 'territorial protectorates' in various parts of the world. This served to expand British sovereignty and the inhabitants of the colonies became subjects of the British Monarch.

The 1950s and 1960s witnessed a massive government campaign to encourage black immigrant workers to the UK, but from the first stages of their arrival, they were perceived both within and outside government as a problem and the government was powerless to deal with the manifestations of racism.

Racism was rife across society as a whole, in work, in housing, and in the educational system, which affected the children of African Caribbean immigrants. It was expected that black people would assimilate and integrate into the British culture. A voluntary organisation, the National Council for Commonwealth Immigrants, and the subsequent Race Relations Board (now the Commission for Racial Equality) were set up for the purpose of helping immigrants to adapt. But as tensions grew, the black community realised that only self-reliance, self-possession and mutual aid would secure their existence within a hostile environment.

Black self-help organisations, however, can be traced to African, Asian and Caribbean overseas students who, in the 1920s, formed the West African Students Union to oppose racial prejudice and colonialism. In 1931, Harold Moody founded the West Indian League of Coloured Peoples which was devoted to the welfare of 'a coloured' people world-wide and to the improvement of relations between the races.

An attempt was made in the Midlands to tackle the problems faced by black immigrants with the formation of the Bristol Colonial Association in 1952, the first voluntary organisation to assist ethnic minorities. Its brief was to help minorities who had settled in Bristol to deal with impending problems associated with their integration into society. The British Caribbean Welfare Services and statutory bodies in Bristol represented the association. The organisation was disbanded in 1957.

Racial hatred and violence in Nottingham and Notting Hill in the late 1950s caused black organisations to divert their focus from welfare issues to more militant campaigning, although both emphases gradually became integral to the black community's strategy for survival in later years.

The West Indian Standing Conference (WISC) was born out of this intense situation in 1959. It is an umbrella organisation of more than two hundred Caribbean individuals and groups who include lawyers, doctors, nurses, teachers, accountants, ministers of religion, social workers, probation officers and small businesses. WISC owes its existence in part to the late Prime Minister of Jamaica, Michael Manley, who in 1958 visited the UK to consult with West Indian community representatives following the outbreak of racial violence. As the longest serving black voluntary body in the UK, the Conference commands respect from governments - nationally and internationally.

Apart from representing broad sectional interests of African Caribbean citizens, WISC supports several initiatives in education, counselling, advocacy, legal advice and research development. A dedicated management committee manages the Conference, whose interests are wide and varied. William Trant OBE was the organisation's Director for several years. He has led campaigns on economic and social justice, as well as equal opportunity policy issues.

Since the 1990s, members have been calling for a change of the name in the organisation. One recommendation was that the Conference should be renamed Standing Conference of Caribbean Organisations. A further suggestion was that the organisation carries the new title of the National Council of Caribbean Organisations (NCCO). The debate on this is set to continue.

Other broad-based community organisations have sprung up as well. The African Caribbean Leadership Council (ACLC) in Hornsey was founded in 1975 in circumstances similar to WISC.

In 1991, the Black Community Forum of Sheffield was established to increase the black community's participation in decision-making, to improve the skills of young people and to encourage various groups to tap into the resources of the city's overall regeneration programme. More than sixty organisations are affiliated to the BCF.

In 1995, the Forum negotiated a highly successful Single Regeneration Bid, which ran into several millions of pounds. It was a credit to the perseverance and unity of Chairman Seaton Gosling and his executive who fought a long battle for their community.

Black voluntary groups fought consistently for quality housing for elderly black people in the UK, especially in largely depressed inner-city areas. Guyanese-born Lee Samuel, MBE, led the way in this respect. A voluntary worker in the field of community relations, she was founder member and chair of the Carib Housing Association.

Carib Housing Association Ltd is a not-for-profit charity founded in 1979 to look after the housing needs of the West Indian elderly that were not catered for by local authorities nor the voluntary sector. The client group included people who suffer loneliness and cultural isolation, lack of family support, inadequate or unsuitable housing conditions and ill treatment by a spouse or relative.

Carib's first housing project was the rehabilitation of a previously dilapidated property - known as Alan Kelly House - in Kensington and Chelsea, which was completed in 1983. The organisation's first newly constructed project was the Clive Lloyd House, which was opened by distinguished cricketer, Clive Lloyd, OBE, in 1985 in Haringey.

Six years on, Carib's flagship project - Lee Samuel House- was opened in June 1991, and named after the Charity's founder. Situated in the heart of Brixton, the building comprises 28 one-bedroom flats. By May 1992, another project - Bishop Wilfred Wood Court in Newham - was launched and named after Carib's President, the Rt. Rev. Wilfred Wood, Bishop of Croydon.

Carib has set a prime example to the black voluntary sector. It was influential in getting public attention towards the acute housing crisis in London. Moreover, the association has shown daring enterprise in a market in which members of the black community were excluded at the time.

The stirring advocacy by other black housing organisations, including the Federation of Black Housing Organisations (FBHO) and Ujima, has influenced a more enlightened community housing policy, which is integrated into urban regeneration schemes throughout England today. FBHO was founded in 1983 at a conference in Reading by black housing workers and others with an interest in housing matters.

Its motto - A better housing deal for Black People - was all embracing. Priorities covered two main issues; firstly, the registration of black housing groups with the Housing Corporation and secondly, increasing the proportion of black staff in housing associations and local authorities.

Ten years later, 50 new black and ethnic minority housing associations were registered.

The organisation has had a creditable record of representing the black community in the area of social housing. The more established black associations have shared the expertise and knowledge with smaller and fewer experienced ones.

Unlike the mainstream voluntary sector, it is the experience of racial hostility that united and drove the black voluntary sector. This helped to shape our history and character, thereby enabling us to be seen as a distinct sector with equal housing needs.

The Black Contractors Association (BCA) was born out of the determination by a group of African and Caribbean builders to gain equal opportunities in the community. Many Caribbean nationals who came to Britain in the 1940s and 1950s came with expert knowledge in joinery, carpentry and the building and construction industry, but alas had to settle for menial work and were deprived of using skills with which they were equipped.

The early pioneers of the BCA were, Mike Harry, Vernon Payne, Chris Francis and Horace Thompson. The association was set up in 1985 as a voluntary organisation to improve the position of black builders and contracting firms in the London Borough of Lambeth and later Southwark. The organisation also aimed to ensure that those builders on the council's List of Approved Contractors received a portion of contracts.

Before the BCA was established, there were only two black contractors in the total of 15 approved by Lambeth. Yet they received a very negligible portion of the work. Most of it was given to white contractors from outside of the borough.

By 1986 the organisation was properly constituted with a full management committee and coordinator, after the famous Lord Scarman Report in 1981, and a study by Lambeth, which identified discrimination, suffered by black people in the labour market.

Between 1988 and 1995, more than 400 firms joined the association. They provided employment for more than 2,000 persons. Training programmes for apprentices as well as business support and advice were offered to members and the general public.

Annual banquets raised the profile of the BCA in the local area. Politicians, trade unionists, celebrities, local authority officials and international guests used such events to help inspire confidence in the black community. A glossy brochure with highly informative and entertaining articles on the housing, construction and related industries complemented the yearly activities of the association.

The BCA gained international recognition in 1994 when a delegation from the United Kingdom attended the 25th conference and celebration of the National Association of Minority Contractors in the US. The US association was impressed by the militancy of their UK counterparts. Collaboration with minority contractors in South Africa was also discussed and later, delegations from the US and South Africa visited Britain.

The civil disturbances in the major inner cities in England, coupled with the Scarman Report, jolted the Conservative Government into action. The thrust towards greater community participation in the decision-making process has been a unique experience for the black voluntary sector. Community business associations founded on the principle of charity or not-for-profit were formed throughout the country.

Former race relations officer, Daoud Laurence, who arrived in England from Dominica in the 1950s, was a founder-member and chair of the Black Business Association (BBA), Waltham Forest, East London in 1987. The African Caribbean community in the borough were under represented in all areas of political and social life. The decline in the furniture trade, engineering and other industries, fuelled staggering unemployment rates especially in the black community. Those who sought self-employment as a viable option encountered much difficulty from mainstream institutions

The BBA's core services were: business support, counselling, training, research and development and advocacy. It was recognised as the lead player in community development by public and private agencies, along with community groups. The BBA was instrumental in the construction of the African-Caribbean Centre in Leyton in the 1980s. It was entirely due however, to Laurence's passionate struggles and the consistency of others that this facility became a reality.

The Bristol Black Business Association was established in 1986. Its objectives were to represent the needs of the black business sector, form links between black businesses, facilitate cross trading between these businesses and to promote the philosophy of enterprise throughout the black community.

Another voluntary organisation that has displayed remarkable resilience is Sia (meaning A force for intelligent thought), which was established in 1985. Sia is a national development agency, which supports the survival and development of black voluntary organisations.

Sia has been involved in high profile events, including the Race for

Justice '95' conference to address issues of concern for African, Caribbean and Asian communities at the Commonwealth Institute. It has supported the setting up of local black development agencies such as the Bristol Black Voluntary Sector Development Unit.

After years of campaigning, a group of energised volunteers, frustrated by the poor treatment meted out to black refugees and immigrants, formed the Caribbean African and Latin American Association (CALA) in September 1989 in Brixton. The principal founders were Mike Graham, Fidel Cordero, Juan Cava, Taata Ofosu, Yen Nyeya, Abdul Raheem and Basil Bollers. The organisation provides technology training to the refugee and immigrant population to gain employment and pursue higher education.

Of course it was not only contractors and other tradesmen/women who found discrimination unpalatable in the job market. Other professions did too. The Society of Black Architects (SOBA) was formed in June 1990 to represent the interests of black men and women in the architectural practice and education. The society campaigns against and challenges racism within the profession and society generally.

SOBA has more than 200 members drawn from architectural practices and educational institutions. In January 1995, the late Bernie Grant, MP, at the request of the organisation, convened a meeting at the House of Commons to focus on the inability of housing associations and voluntary bodies to implement equal opportunity policies and commission Black Architectural Practices.

Project Fullemploy, a national charity with central government support, was set up in 1992 in east London with a mission to help remove some of the barriers preventing the black community from making the transition into positions of management in the country's mainstream activities. This has been a very positive step forward and the results are encouraging.

Clearly, from the foregoing progress has been made, but not without hard work and determination of hard-nosed voluntary workers cum entrepreneurs set on changing the status of blacks and improving the playing field for the community.

Jeremy Crook, a young and inspiring leader, is director of the Black Training & Enterprise Group (BTEG), which advocates self-help strategies to stimulate growth in black communities through training and enterprise activities.

Crook has produced well-researched policy documents on: Investing in Black People, the Black Voluntary Sector Manifesto and The Black

Economy.

The black voluntary sector's contribution to the development of arts and culture is very substantial. This area of enterprise is often taken for granted by the host community and also to a large extent the immigrant population as well. This situation is a direct result of its negative portrayal by the mass media.

In December 1988, The 198 Gallery was opened to showcase the work of Africa, Caribbean and Asian artists in south London. It was founded by Clarence Thompson, chairman; Zoe Linsley-Thomas, administrator; and Devon C. Thomas, business and marketing manager. The gallery is a registered charity with a solid management board drawn from leaders of the black community and young, professional artists. The organisation was earmarked to become a National Vocational Qualification (NVQ) Assessment Centre for the Cultural Industries in late 1997.

Another initiative, which evolved as a result of pressures from the local community, was the Global Trade Centre (GTC) in North London. The irrepressible late Tottenham MP, Bernie Grant, on 9th September 1997, launched it.

The centre seeks to capitalise on the strategic link which minority ethnic groups have with their countries of origin - encompassing culture, language and informal networks.

These contacts and other local resources are used to promote trade between small and medium sized businesses in North London, Africa and the Caribbean. It is hoped that there will be greater economic activity in trade, which is certain to generate new employment opportunities for the wider community.

The black voluntary sector, in time, with its sound foundations is poised without doubt to make a difference in the black community and national productivity.

Law & Politics

English people had a profound belief that every Nigerian was a lawyer or the son of a chief. That was probably reflective of a truism. Before the black population became a perceived problem, those who interacted with the indigenous population, apart from West Indian sportsmen and entertainers, were of high standing who came to complete their studies or seek a better way of life. This chapter will therefore, illustrate the achievements of African Caribbean people in the fields of law and politics.

Buoyed by British colonialism, sons of middle-class families, especially in Africa, the Caribbean and the Indian sub-continent, sought opportunities for advancement through the legal system and other academic routes. Many used law as a career to politics, particularly in Local Government. During the post-war period, people of colour used both America and Britain as the launching pad for political independence and internal self-government in their respective lands.

However, there were profound differences between the comparatively well off and the impoverished, poorly educated immigrants who found themselves at the mercy of a system they did not understand. In the two decades immediately after the Second World War, it was difficult for an established solicitor to appreciate social disadvantage; moreso, ignorance of one's constitutional rights, and not having the slightest idea of how to redress this injustice. The new arrivals suffered deplorable employment and housing conditions in the absence of professional advice. Much later, this situation gradually changed, as the African Caribbeans made their presence felt in the system.

Trinidadian Erwin Ewart Adams was called to the Bar in 1970. He attended the University of the West Indies (UWI) and lectured in both Jamaica and Trinidad. He was a member of the National Council for Civil Liberties and worked at free advice centres in the major cities of Britain. Guyanese Moses Kempadoo served as a solicitor after studying at the University of London. He worked with the social services organisation in the London Borough of Lambeth, South London. His cultural pursuits included his chairmanship of the London Guyanese Dramatic Society. Today he and his wife are actively involved in economic and social development programmes in Africa.

Another Guyanese, Harry Narayan, arrived in the early 1960s and attended Lincoln's Inn. He became a barrister, and was part of the West Indian League and the Brixton Neighbourhood Community Association. Bruce Pitt, son of the late Lord Pitt, studied at the University of London before moving to Gray's Inn. While still in his twenties, he became involved in social work, including the Harambee Project and the South London Parents Association. In these formative years, voluntary legal assistance was vital to the progress of all community organisations.

Lensworth Small who was born in Spanish Town, Jamaica, was called to the Bar, but later became a solicitor. For years, he held a very high profile in Brixton where he expressed a passion for supporting the educationally sub-normal, including the disaffected young. He was one of few professionals who advocated that youths born to Caribbean parents should remain in Britain rather than return to their parents homeland. He insisted that the community should be organised effectively to meet this challenge. This fact is so obvious now, though it was not apparent at the time. Small also provided advice through the pages of the Jamaican weekly Gleaner newspaper.

The law touches all aspects of life, and Caribbean people are to be found in its many areas. Joycelyn Gibbs is a celebrated specialist in the family division of the courts, whereas Anesta Weeks, a Barrister of Montserratian parentage, is a specialist in employment law.

Hilda Amoo-Gottfried was a barrister for ten years before becoming a solicitor. She is a member of the Law Society, including that organisation's Race Relations Committee and Women's Careers Working Party. Councillor Kofi Appiah, who was born in Ghana, obtained a law degree from the University of London and was called to the Bar in the early 1970s. He is a member of the Inner Temple and was formerly Assistant State Attorney in Ghana. Councillor Hazel Baird is another lawyer involved with local government. She chaired the Brent Women's Committee, as well as the governing body of the Willesden College of Technology.

Delano Frank Bart was called to the Bar in 1977. He was an executive member of the Society of Black Lawyers and the Afro-Caribbean Medical Society. Bart is a member of the South Bank Polytechnic Minority Access to the Legal Profession Project and of WISC. Barrister Edmund Cofie is also an executive member of the Society of Black Lawyers (SBL) and serves on the management committee of the North Kensington Law Centre. Andrew Gumbiti-Zimuto, who is also a barrister-member of the SBL, attended the University of Sussex and graduated from the Inns of Court Law School.

Barbadian Sylvia Denman studied law at the University of London and took up a fellowship at the New York University before becoming an academic lawyer at the South Bank Polytechnic in London. Donald Herbert was called to the Bar in 1982, and became vice-chair of the SBL and an executive officer with Lawyers Against Apartheid. He campaigned strenuously for the introduction of anti-racist training for all judges and magistrates, and expressed concern at the disparity in treatment and sentencing between black and white offenders in the criminal justice system.

Barrister Michael Magloire, who was born in St. Lucia, specialises in criminal, family, industrial relations and housing law respectively. He held many positions in local government politics: Chair of the Housing Committee in Brent, member of the SBL and of the Haldane Society of Socialist Lawyers. Brenton Mitchell had a career in business before qualifying as a barrister. His many memberships include the Parole Board, the Police Complaints Board, the Rent Tribunal, WISC, SBL, the Joint Committee Against Racialism and the British Society of Criminology and the Institute of Marketing.

Barrister William Panton chaired the SBL from 1984 to 1987 and the Lewisham Way Youth and Community Centre. He was also the treasurer of the African Caribbean Education Research Project. Councillor Jacob Siaw of Hackney is a lawyer who was previously a headmaster. Martha Osamor is another North London councillor with experience as a legal adviser of the Tottenham Neighbourhood Law Centre, specialising in cases relevant to youth and immigration. Ms Osamor has been involved in the formation of the United Women's Action Group, Haringey Black Pressure Group on Education, Haringey's Black Women's Centre and the Broadwater Farm Youth Association (and Day Centre and Mother's Project). She also chaired the Haringey Independent Police Committee.

Cordella Stewart from Jamaica was admitted as a solicitor in 1987. She is a founder member of the SBL and member of the Minority Access to the Legal Profession Project based at the South Bank Polytechnic (now South Bank University). She is legal adviser to the Broadwater Farm Defence Committee, the Extended Family Housing Association and the Caribbean Hospital Support Group. Alphonso Wynter was admitted as a solicitor in 1984 and is a member of the Law Society and the SBL.

Noteworthy African Caribbean legal practitioners who suffered injustices of one type or another sought to establish independent organisations to help fellow immigrants and even those from the indigenous population. One such reputable organisation was Black Rights (UK), established in 1982, following the Lord Scarman Inquiry into the disturbances in Brixton the previous year. Guyanese Roy Sawh, known mostly for his anti-racist campaigns at Hyde Park Corner during the 1960s, was the organisation's first director, while the erudite legal brain, was the late Rudy Narayan. The proactive Sam Springer served as co-chairman. In addition to campaigning on issues specially related to the black community, the Society pressed for the fusion of the barrister and solicitor professions, the provision of a national Bill of Rights and a general improvement of the legal service.

Black Rights established an advice centre and received a substantial amount of enquiries, which led to the passing of the Nationality Act on the first day of 1988. Another Guyanese, Harold Mangar, succeeded Sawh as director, with Harold Alleyne as administrative secretary. The former was seconded from the Commission for Racial Equality. At the time he was Senior Projects and Training Officer, while previously (between 1969 - 1977), he served as Conciliation Officer Secretary to the South Metropolitan Committee at the Race Relations Board. Mangar obtained a certificate in Industrial Relations and Trade Union Law from the London School of Economics.

The injustices that the African Caribbean population experienced were publicised, with some being controversial, politically. Yet other cases remained unpublished and in many instances, the African Caribbean community suffered tremendously. Immigrants were generally ignorant about both the law and the institutions which were established to represent them. Little wonder organisations like Black Rights (UK) and the persons associated with it, including the fiery Narayan, suffered at the hands of the Establishment.

Narayan, who was director of the Society, was criticised repeatedly for his combative style of advocacy. His frequent appearance as spokesperson for the black community, with or without permission, is immaterial. The controversial nature of his campaigns however, is not the issue. The mere presence of a black lawyer in the public eye - whatever his demeanour - was some consolation to people who were too apprehensive to use the formal legal system. Black Rights (UK) was therefore essential to the community relations industry and today it spawns a network of allied services: legal advocacy, immigration, citizens advice bureau, all of which were inclusive functions of local government agencies.

Shortly after arriving in Britain, Narayan worked at washing dishes in Lyons cornershops and packing Brillo soap-pads to finance his law studies. He learnt much also from military service. He was the founder and first president of the students union at Lincoln's Inn. He was renowned for his brilliant oratorical and debating skills at that legal institution. He claims to have been inspired by former world heavy weight champion Muhammad Ali's exemplary commitment to his people. In 1969, Narayan joined the late Courtney Laws in setting up the legal section of the Brixton Neighbourhood Community Association. From there Narayan went to work with Tony Mohipp and Rhodan Gordon at the Black Peoples Information Centre where he started an advice section with Jimmy Fairweather and co-operated with Guy Elliston, Asquith Gibbes and John Chevvannes in other boroughs. He participated in similar community projects in Birmingham. A feature of the centre was the presence of black staff, thus giving visitors a sense of belonging and confidence. Narayan became chairman of WISC's legal panel and served on committees of the Race Relations Board.

After three decades of involvement in the community's legal life, barrister Narayan has many achievements to his credit, including his integral part in the foundation of the SBL and Black Rights (UK), and authorship of 'Barrister for the Defence' published in 1985. So popular were his campaigns, that matters relating to law in the black community generally, are attributed to him. Perhaps like Narayan, former English fast bowler, Freddie Truman is typified when the game of cricket is discussed by the older generation who have a passionate loyalty for English cricket.

During the 19th and 20th centuries, our contribution to political mainstream in Britain was as infectious as the bubonic plague during the First World War. Randolph Beresford, MBE, BEM, became the first Caribbean-born Mayor of a London Borough (Hammersmith & Fulham) in 1976. Despite the colour bar, Caribbean professionals used their intellectual gifts and negotiating skills to charter into political waters, during the establishment. As it turned out, the late Dr David Pitt and cricket legend, Learie Constantine, became two of the first peers in the House of Lords. Since the last half of the 20th century and the beginning of the 21st century, under the Labour Government, Caribbean peers have mushroomed; namely, Baroness Patricia Scotland of Ashtal in Oxfordshire, who is a junior minister and Lord Waheed Alli of Norbury, the youngest member of the House of Lords, both of whom have reached the proverbial apex of power.

Two Guyanese professionals have been fast tracked in the national political system. Baroness Valerie Amos, a well-known dedicated equalities specialist, has moved swiftly up the political ladder from a mere junior Foreign Office Minister to more recently, International Secretary, being the most senior Black female Labour Cabinet appointment in the history of any British Government. Her secret code is "It is always useful to know one's history. I think that it is important to be clear about the values and principles which underpin one's life."

David Lammy who succeeded the late Bernie Grant, MP in the Tottenham Constituency is now a Junior Health Minister, with another brilliant barrister, Paul Boateng, appointed the position of Chief Secretary to the Treasury - the third in line in that particular department.

Lord Herman Ouseley's meteoric rise to fame is also a rarity. Undoubtedly, he is the exponent on Race Relations in Britain, as well as Europe. As a consequence, his inimitable style is a cause for much comfort and pride.

Dianne Abbott and Bernie Grant (now deceased) were among the first black MPs to be appointed in 1987, Abbott being the first black woman MP to this prestigious position. We also have Baroness Ros Howells who has been elevated to the House of Lords. At the local government level, while there remain a disproportionate number of Black councillors, in recent times, there have been elections for Caribbean Mayors and Mayoresses. While the colour bar still remains a negotiating factor in the equation of British power politics, Caribbean people are gradually finding a route towards mainstream politics.

In summing up the practicalities of the Caribbean Lordship system, one leader writer was forced to genuflect this way: "It was hard to imagine Caribbean immigrants would scale the heights of the Motherland. But with the beach-head they have now on Mount Lords, they are well on the way to getting to that very summit."

While many black people consider themselves as victims of discrimination and prejudice, community lawyers have boosted their confidence in the British legal system by succeeding in high profile cases. Those who are therefore involved at various levels of the legal and associated professions should be commended for their courage and dedication towards social justice. Inevitably, some worthy persons will be overlooked, and in this instance, I hope they do not institute legal proceedings against me for biographical negligence.

Sport

Even the most fervent of racists would concede that black people are good at sport. We play cricket brilliantly, box with panache and power, run swiftly and excel at every other physical activity -well, at least some of us do. The trouble is that our general performance in the sporting world has blinded others to our real achievements. There is no denying that the white community is aware of the brilliance of our sportsmen and women - past and present - long before they knew us as neighbours.

The first immigrants who settled in Britain originated from Africa and the Caribbean. They included seamen, servants, and runaway slaves. Very few employment opportunities were available to them. Manual labour required skills similar to those of the navy, boxing, athletics and entertainment. These skills ranged from agility and flexibility to physical strength.

Those who defended themselves successfully against racial aggression or remained deficient in the midst of an extremely hostile environment were best adept at using their fists to make a meagre living. Just as how slaves in Ancient Rome achieved fame and modest comfort as gladiators, so the itinerant, rootless black male was publicly acclaimed in the boxing ring.

Cricketing skills were the preserve of the sporting gentry with a clear dividing line as to who could be admitted to share in this elite past-time. By the 19th century, cricket had spread from the countryside into the towns. African Caribbean people copied the game from their colonial masters adding subtle polish and technique, which were to make champions of erstwhile underlings. Unlike other occurrences, cricket was not linked to mass migration from the Caribbean later in this century. G. Elliot is recorded as having scored 117 not out for a West Indies team against Tufnell Park back in 1889. There is little doubt that the embryonic community was awe-inspired by stories of sporting success with respect to other races elsewhere. Tom Molyneaux and Bill Richmond were two of the first African-American boxers to visit Britain. The cricket tours by the Australian aborigines and the Parsis from India over a hundred years ago may have been remote, but C.A. Oliverre, a batsman from St. Vincent, made such an impression on the visit in 1900, that he was invited to stay on to play for Derbyshire in the County Championship.

Such achievements were mere dreams for most people - they were too busy keeping body and soul together. For all races in previous generations, sport was mainly a hobby for the well to do rather than a daily profession. It was even worse for the average working class or the grassroots of society. Sporting life was more liberal than other strands of society whose attitude was to shun the unfortunate and the deprived. If a man could entertain by running fast, jumping high, hitting a ball or knocking someone flat - and for as long as he could do so - society was prepared to overlook insignificant matters such as whether the person had a criminal record, was of working class background or even black.

Indeed, racism was just as entrenched in sport as any other social activity. Yet other factors were more important in the arena. A participant's worth was measured by the extent to which he could excite spectators or make money for his patrons. However, while some sporting clubs continued to impose the colour bar, others were reluctant to do so.

The first African-Caribbean boxers and cricketers were welcomed as providers of the so-called 'glamorous entertainment', providing they did not defeat the local heroes. These men were true ambassadors of their race. They offered spectators and followers of the sport a chance to witness the way of life and achievements of the black community. Learie Constantine and Larry Gains became celebrities. Trinidadian Constantine, in particular, was a classic and exciting post-war cricket all-rounder. His later work in social welfare in Britain earned him a well-deserved knighthood. Through his fine example, he elevated the Caribbean society to further recognition.

Contact in sport travelled along the parallel lines of public schools, middle-class professions, and mobile tradesmen such as master masons, sailors, soldiers, carpenters and canal-diggers. Seamen and the military, both officers and lower ranks, were credited for taking cricket and other sports to the various colonies of the then British Empire.

Although cricket became one of the pivotal regional institutions, the West Indies did not compete as an international entity until around the Second World War. Earlier teams comprised gentlemen of the plantocracy and administrators, augmented by a few black professionals who were granted leave from work. Yet in the Caribbean territories there was a wealth of enthusiasm and talent in the clubs that could spawn succeeding generations of sportsmen and women. The late Sir Frank Worrell was the first black captain of the West Indies cricket team, breaking the cycle of the white mercantile class. He was followed later (in the 1970s and 1980s) by Sir

Garfield Sobers, Rohan Kanhai and Clive Lloyd. The latter was the longest serving cricket captain in the world (from 1974 - 1984).

Gary Gains was good enough to beat two future world heavyweight champions and would have fought for the crown if the image of Jack Johnson, a bogeyman to the sporting establishment, was not imprinted on the professional sport. In 1931 Gains defeated Phil Scott of Leicester for the Commonwealth heavyweight title. He lost the title after three successful defences against British Len Harvey.

During this period, black boxers were considered only sparring partners. Yolande Pompey was the first West Indian considered good enough to challenge for world honours. Some shrewd judges believe that Pompey was pushed, rather than placed, into battle with the legendary Archie Moore.

Jamaican Joe Bygraves won the Commonwealth heavy weight title in 1956. A year later, he pulverised Britain's best-loved fighter, Henry Cooper, in nine rounds. Bygraves was not allowed to fight for the British title, as no foreigners were given that chance. Later that rule was relaxed to a ten-year residency period.

Bunny Sterling became the first black migrant to win a British title in 1970, when he beat Mark Rowe for the middleweight crown. Maurice Hope, who achieved European honours, gained the middleweight world title in 1979. When the history of black British fighters is written, Hope will secure for himself a prominent place. He was a true pioneer of the game.

Cliff Anderson, Kid Tanner and Roy Ankrah participated in the explosion of interest in the 1940s which led to the success of Hogan Bassey and Dick Tiger, thereby paving the way for another generation of boxers such as Lloyd Honeygan and Frank Bruno.

Football took longer to attract the African Caribbean community. By force of circumstances, minorities have to excel individually rather than at team sports. Cricket, incidentally, is a team sport played by individuals. Nevertheless, it was inevitable that the growing inner-city population would one day penetrate the essentially urban activity of football.

The stimulus came from outside, however. The Brazilians, who dominated world soccer from the late 1950s, and especially the incomparable Pele, inspired confidence and emulation like the West Indian cricketers. Even so, Eusebio, who was forgotten earlier, demonstrated through stunning performances for Portugal in the World Cup played in England in 1966, what black footballers could achieve in a predominantly white team. We should not forget Britain's first professional outfield black footballer, Walter Tull, who was also the first black soldier in 1916. He played for Spurs and Northampton between 1909 and 1914. He was killed in action during the First World War, aged 29. At the time of writing, the Walter Tull Memorial Gardens with a centrepiece statute was scheduled to be opened in late 1997.

Lindy Delaphena had played in the championship-winning Portsmouth team in 1948, and comedian Charlie Williams was active in the lower divisions of the Football League. The real advance coincided with the appearance of Clyde Best for West Ham in the late 1960s and reached avalanche proportions a decade later with the arrival of Laurie Conningham, Viv Anderson and Luther Blissett. By the time John Barnes became a national hero, there were African Caribbean footballers at all levels of the game. Since then, other players like Les Ferdinand, Paul Ince and Ian Wright have come to dominate the sport with scintillating performances. The commercial stakes of the game became of such that in January 1995 Andy Cole was involved in a record transfer from Newcastle to Manchester United for £7.5 million.

The astute and tactical Ruud Gullit had clearly transformed Chelsea Football Club into a winning side. The black Dutch player-manager is considered one of the most successful football administrators in Britain, if not Europe.

The British Rugby Union is associated with public schools, universities and such other traditional institutions. It may come as a surprise to learn that Jim Peters represented England in 1906. Inevitably he was dubbed *"Darkie"*, but at least he was given the chance to play. There was no footballer of similar high profile in the amateur league until Cris Oti made an impressionable debut in 1988.

Professional Rugby League draws from a wider cross-section of the community, primarily in the working-class industrial towns of northern England. Billy Boston is regarded as one of its greatest players. Clive Sullivan led Great Britain to World Cup triumph in the 1970s. Ellery Hanley has become the League's best-known personality in a team which also included Desmond Drummond, Henderson Gill and Martin Offiah. West Indians have been part of the English County Cricket Championship since the early years of the century, but they tended to come direct from the region rather than from the community established here. Roland Butcher was the first African Caribbean to play for England in 1981. He came from Middlesex, which draws on the substantial population of North and West London. Club colleagues, Norman Cowans and Wilfred Slack, also followed in the footsteps of Butcher.

Before the county championship was opened to them in 1968, leading Caribbean cricketers earned their professional status in the Northern leagues.

Constantine, when elevated to the nobility, considered himself very much at home on both sides of the Atlantic. Similarly, Barbadian-born Gordon Greenidge who grew up in Reading enjoyed playing for both the West Indies and his county, Hampshire. Along with the brilliant South-African opening batsman Barry Richards (now retired from the game), Greenidge shared in record-breaking partnerships throughout much of the 1970s and 1980s, especially for Hampshire. Later Greenidge and his fellow Barbadian, Desmond Haynes, became the most durable opening batting pair in the history of Test cricket.

In July 1994, the Caribbean Times newspaper reported that the 'Knives are out for West Indian geniuses in county cricket'. The articles were in response to the proposed ban on overseas players by the English Test and County Cricket Board. There has long been a bitter resentment in some circles over the dominance of English cricket by the largely talented West Indians.

As far back as the mid-20th century the late Sir Frank Worrell, that master-tactician, played for Lancashire for twelve years, earning from the start £500 yearly - a princely sum in those days.

Many years later, Lloyd, with his dashing strokeplay, and Michael Holding with his Rolls-Royce bowling, made their county one of the strongest in the country. The contribution of Andy Roberts, Gordon Greenidge and later, Malcolm Marshall, made their respective counties financially viable, after the counties were teetering on the edge.

Apart from building the coffers of counties, overseas players in general have revolutionised British cricket. While the English have tried to perfect technical precision in batsmanship for example, foreign players have combined technique with breath-taking enterprise.

Even so, Greenidge's successors, whether they were born in Britain or arrived as children from the Caribbean, did not have that choice - for better for worse - their sporting future lay with England.

It is interesting to note that most of these cricketers spent their formative years in provincial or suburban areas rather than in the big cities - Butcher from Stevenage, Slack from High Wycombe, Phillip de Freitas and Martin Jean-Jacques from London's western edge, Cardigan Connor from Slough and Greenidge from Reading. Most of these cricketers (with the exception of Greenidge himself) have originated from the small Eastern Caribbean states as against the bigger territories of the region.

Unlike the West Indies where cricket is played in both the city and the countryside (not forgetting that some of our famous stars have come from urban slums), the sport is a rural one in England. This explains the reason why most African Caribbean youths are not attracted to the game, since they reside in the larger metropolitan centres. There are several economic and social reasons for this situation.

The emphasis on comprehensive education has weakened the former association with the national (Grammar) school curriculum, in which sport played a significant part. Greater attention is now given to individual participation in major spectator sports, and education theorists are less keen on the competitive aspect. Because of inadequate space and scarce resources, established clubs have sited their cricket fields away from the heart of the cities.

The young West Indian learning the game with a makeshift bat and ball is a clichè, but it is true nonetheless. His cousin in London, Birmingham or Manchester lives among high-rise flats which prohibit ball games.

The black community has shown considerable enterprise by developing alternative sporting activities which require minimum space or expenditure on equipment. Laurie Ince has blended martial arts disciplines with entertainment in funding the 'Sam Tu Dang Society'. Membership is open to all young people wanting to develop skills in self-defence. The sport/ self defence package is widespread, appealing to contemporary urban life.

The creation of specialist sporting schools of excellence is evolving all the time. The London Cricket College (formerly the Haringey Cricket College in Tottenham) is pioneering this vision. Former West Indian cricketer, Reggie Scarlett, is co-director of the academy. Through his inspiration, dozens of youngsters are now competent enough to be signed up by various counties.

The Sports Council, Haringey Council and the Tottenham Grammar School Foundation modestly fund the centre. The institution is universally respected, especially as patrons include Sir Colin Cowdrey, Graham Gooch and rock icons, Mick Jagger and Bill Wyman.

The cricket academy has a melting pot of ethnic cultures. Training is divided between playing cricket, coaching in schools and formal tuition, mainly in maths and English. Scarlett played alongside Sobers and Worrell as an all-rounder in the 1960 West Indian team against England.

So successful is Scarlett's project that it is the model for an Australian cricket academy, which has already produced Australian wrist spinner, Shane Warne and West Indies skipper, Carl Hooper. Despite limited resources, the indomitable will of Scarlett and his assistant has prevailed.

Clive Myers, a wrestler known to millions through television, learned the same discipline. He pioneered arm-wrestling as a basic, but universal pastime in which everyone can compete, irrespective of race, affluence, social class, or disability. Myers achieved a major breakthrough by bringing the world's arm-wrestling championships - male and female - to Britain.

Other sports such as basketball generated interest by media (especially television) coverage of the sport in which African-Americans excel. Sports organisations in inner cities and local authorities have encouraged youths to participate in a range of other non-traditional sports, including street-hockey. It remains to be seen whether such innovations will develop alongside the more traditional games in Britain.

Over the last decade, African-Caribbean athletes have attained universal success in track and field events. Sprinters of West Indian descent, for instance, dominate the British and Canadian teams as well as those from the home territories. Linford Christie is amongst the greatest living sprinters in world athletics today. Canadian Ben Johnson, whose movement resembled that of a gazelle, was banned from active competition after he was tested for doping, a practice that is widespread among athletes of all descriptions. Yet Johnson's phenomenal success in the 1980s and early 1990s still lingers in the minds of the universal sporting public.

The fact is that West Indians have an excellent record in international sporting competition. Jamaicans, for example, were the stars of the immediate post-war era. George Rhoden, Arthur Wint, Leslie Laing and Herb McKenley comprised the record-breaking 4 x 400 metres relay team which took the gold medal in the 1952 Olympics at Helsinki. Wint, McKenley and Emmanuel McDonald Bailey, a Trinidadian based in Britain, were the individual heroes there and in London four years earlier.

The intensity of television coverage of the 1968 Olympics in Mexico, and the brouhaha surrounding the 'Black Power' demonstration, sparked interest with the generation who claimed honours two decades later. Marilyn Neufville caused controversy when she elected to represent Jamaica after making her reputation in Britain.

Decathlon Daley Thompson, javelin-thrower Tessa Sanderson and others - Sonia Lannaman, Judy Simpson, Kris Akabussi, John Herbert, Mick McFarlane, Heather Oakes, Beverly Kinch, Colin Jackson, Denise Lewis (now headhunted as a sporting beauty queen because of her charming personality) and relay specialist, Phil Brown - are all class acts. Jackson retired from athletics in March 2003 after more than fifteen years as the British hurdles champion. African-Caribbean athletes have played an important role in standards of excellence, especially in indoor competitions. Some are still under the glare of the media, especially television. Akabussi for instance, is an accomplished television presenter.

Sanderson is an outstanding sports ambassador for the black community in Britain. She was awarded the MBE in 1985 in recognition of her services to sport and, that same year, she was given a Hansib Community award. She also holds an Honorary Fellowship from the University of Wolverhampton and an Honorary Masters Degree from Birmingham University.

Her promotional activities include presenting and appearing on network television and radio. In 1988, Tessa worked for two and a half years as a sports presenter for Sky News.

She is involved in charitable work for the Variety Club, Great Ormond Street Hospital, and the Paul Orgorman Leukaemia Fund. In 1993 she launched her own designer leisure wear and exercise video under the title *Body Blitz*. She was voted athlete of the Year for three years by the Sports Writers' Association and Sports Personality of the Year by the Athletics Writers' Association. Her athletics career spanned 19 years - 1973 to 1992. In the latter year she took first place representing Europe in the World Cup Javelin tournament in Cuba.

While we enjoy the glitter, the glamour and receive a measure of compensation in the respective sporting departments, the issue still remains that we do not have many black sports administrators, including promoters, in direct proportion to our African American counterparts.

Our sportsmen and women suffer the effects of economic and social deprivation in the community. It goes without saying that in their formative years, they suffered disproportionately from inadequate facilities and found it impossible to secure sponsorship even when they attained stardom. The implications go further than that which permeate the entire sporting realm.

Boxing promoters give priority to the numbers of tickets sold to ensure sport's viability. The hefty price of tickets prevents the majority of black supporters from attending various bouts to give moral support to their heroes. On the other hand, black boxers with little opportunity to earn a decent living were prepared to be last-minute substitutes to boost the record of a local pugilist.

African Caribbean people, in general, do not support County cricket, even if the match between Hampshire and Middlesex included exciting stars such as the late Malcolm Marshall, Greenidge, Butcher, Cowans, Slack and Wayne Daniel (most of whom have retired from the game). The most experienced and dominant West Indian players were former territorial representatives of the 1960s period. Spectators who attend West Indian club one-day and three-day competitions are therefore mostly middle-aged. In recent years, their support has been dwindling.

Test matches are a different matter. The attraction can best be described as more nostalgic and related to national identity, although the recent series between England and the West Indies underlined the difference between the fathers who considered themselves to be primarily West Indian and attended, and sons who felt strongly they are firstly Black Britons and stayed away.

Yet, there are other sporting activities, which interest West Indians. Horseracing is an obsession in Jamaica, as well as in Trinidad and Tobago, but West Indian attendance at English races is negligible. This of course is a different sporting environment - affluent, aristocratic and far removed from the inner cities.

The African Caribbean community expresses its passion for the turf, but mainly by gambling in betting shops throughout the country. It would be true to say that the playing field is much more open today than it was in the recent past and black sportsmen and women are better rewarded for their efforts.

It is also noticeable that commercial sponsorship has added a new dimension to sports persons earnings. Football and boxing have led the way in this development. Positive change in sport is also taking place in the areas of management. Black promoters, managers, trainers and referees are welcome indicators. The rise of Ambrose Mendy, for example, as a boxing promoter and the varied management skills of ex-footballer Garth Crooks bodes well for the community.

The black community can also take comfort in the fact that many of our great sporting heroes have become entrepreneurs of no mean order. These include names such as Malcolm Marshall and Joel Garner, for instance, who are engaged in the manufacturing of footwear and brand sponsorship, while others hold company directorships globally.

In the boxing fraternity, however, it is heavyweight boxer Lennox Lewis who has been more proactive. In 1996 he led the way in the establishment of the Lennox Lewis College in North London. The institution will train youths in a range of technical and vocational skills to prepare them for the world of work. His initiative is timely and sets a fine example for others to follow.

Sport is a great unifying force for nations, for communities and an unsurpassed source of enjoyment for sports lovers the world over.

West Indian cricket has done more in uniting the region than anything else. Worrell engineered the spirit harmony, Sobers consolidated it, Lloyd fused a fighting-machine and Richards gave it form. Through their exploits (unlike our political leaders), the West Indian cricketers have taught us that regional harmonious integration is possible, if the will is summoned. I cannot help but refer to the sporting glamour and the achievements of "The Greatest" and to what Muhammad Ali meant to people all over the world. Carl Lewis has inspired a similar loyalty - though briefly checked by the hungry sprinter, Ben Johnson - another athlete with more direct Caribbean connection. Ruud Gullit, the Dutch footballer/player at Chelsea, has shown that, apart from North America, we have international heroes from Europe as well. Player identification or adulation begins at the club level. Many teams have a number of African Caribbean players and this led to the West Ham hooligan element, which was once anti-black, being overtaken and the abuse directed against the National Front supporters. Through this development, loyal support for John Barnes and the England team grew astonishingly.

Since black players invaded English football in the late 1970s, they have always been present in international squads. Paul Ince became the first Black player to captain the international side in 1994, while Ian Wright was an extraordinary football legend. Sports writer Al Hamilton argues that a black English squad is capable of frightening any international side in the world.

Young people have also been inspired by successes in the non-traditional sporting events. The victories at karate championships involving Vic Charles and Geoff Thompson popularised the game. Bodybuilder Ian Dowe, following the footsteps of Wilfred Sylvester and Bertil Fox, proved that with discipline, application and training, international honours and respect could be had.

The community is now engaging in almost every area of sport and is a great credit to the nation.

Jamaican Deta Hedman, a furniture assembler from Essex, is arguably the greatest female darts player of all time but is unknown to many. She quit this male-dominated sport in early 1997, after being disillusioned with only winning a string of titles, and not being compensated financially. She hopes to pursue another pastime and has chosen golf as her next challenge.

Undoubtedly, the black community can be justly proud of its great sporting achievement, having set high standards for generations to follow, in the process.

Literature & The Arts

When Trinidadian political activist and writer C.L.R. James died in 1989, several impressive obituaries appeared in various publications, paying homage to his enormous contribution to history, politics, literature and sports. His unique achievement however, has seldom been mentioned in literary reviews. That this Caribbean icon excelled in different fields, is indicative of the originality and creativity of West Indian self-expression which has been directed into specialised channels, and which is in conformity with the more established societies.

Because Caribbean writers, especially, have the vision and the opportunity to travel and are less inclined than most to settle in one place permanently, there is no clear distinction between West Indian literature and black British literature. The early generation of writers in the 20th century worked from England where publishers were accessible and where writers interfaced with each other. Yet they chose to write mainly about the West Indies and, in many cases, for the region's population. Trinidadian writers have a passion for the classics and a desire for literary expression.

In the flowering of talent in the years on either side of 1960, V.S. Naipaul achieved international acclaim for his prize-winning novel, 'A House for Mr. Biswas'. C.L.R James wrote 'The Black Jacobins,' which became an instant classic on black history and literature. 'Beyond the Boundary' is still rated as the best book on cricket (*"what do they know of cricket who only cricket know"*). It is a unique historical study of cricket, as a social and cultural form, which is in part a sustained attempt to repair this neglect. Only the late Jamaican Prime Minister, Michael Manley's, refreshing 'History of West Indian Cricket', equalled this classic. Dramatist Errol John, whose father was a famous cricketer, and whose brother (they were both called George) played a pivotal role in Caribbean journalism, also made an impact on literary development in the black community.

James had an itinerant career. He left his homeland in the early 1930s and made his name as a journalist in England covering cricket, before spending a number of years in the US. As an avowed Pan-Africanist, he worked for some time with the late President of Ghana, Dr. Kwame Nkrumah. When James returned to Britain, he was one of few remaining Marxist ideologues associated with American lawyer, singer and civil rights activist, Paul Robeson, in the years leading up to the outbreak of the Second

World War. James spent his later years in Railton Road, Brixton, which after the events of 1981 became the 'frontline'. As a great literary genius of the century, James' works have not only attracted fellow West Indians, but recently, sections of the European intellectual community who have analysed his works in the context of modern times.

Another Trinidadian of Caribbean classics was Earl Lovelace who won the 1997 prestigious Commonwealth Writers Prize for his latest novel, 'Salt'. The judges described the book as "*a Caribbean novel of huge vigour and vitality, written with dazzling energy.*"

In writing this chapter on literature - the written word - I am reminded that this book itself is concerned mainly with black enterprise in the United Kingdom, and this includes our contribution to the universal intellectual sphere, sometimes referred to as the 'intellectual enterprise'. Deriving from their colonial history, the Caribbean and the greater part of continental Africa have various dialects. The Spanish, French and Dutch-speaking communities have English as their mother tongue. To give justice, therefore, to such interesting developments will require elaboration which this chapter cannot fulfil.

Professor John Figueroa too, combined literature and a love of cricket. He is a distinguished academic. In his book 'Through the Caribbean' Alan Ross described the Professor as "*that Johnsonian, extravagantly-bearded figure, John Figueroa, poet, professor, educationist.*" The Professor has taught and lectured in Jamaica, the US, West Africa and Britain. He is a popular commentator wherever the West Indian cricket team play. Recently, he settled at Milton Keynes close to the Open University.

Black actors and actresses, though excelling in the works of Jean Genet and the Shakespearean classics, have been hampered for years by the lack of dramatists, producers and directors from their own community. That situation changed somewhat when persons such as Michael Abbensetts, Mustapha Matura and Barry Reckford, became part of a growing artistic tradition in Britain. 'Calypso', a play in 1948 by Hedley Briggs with music and lyrics by Ronnie Hill, was accredited as the first true West Indian play in London.

Edric Connor, who died prematurely twenty years later, starred in this play, and his multi-faceted career as an actor, singer, author, composer, producer for film and television and broadcaster, represented several landmarks in stage productions, including *Junction Village* by Douglas Archibald presented on the same bill with his own *Caribbean Revue* medley of music, dance and spectacle. At the time, the Trinidadian was almost alone in maintaining the spirit of West Indian drama in Britain, though the year before he died, BBC television gave impetus to potential artists by encouraging new talent in the Rainbow City series.

There were other important developments in the early 1970s. Barry Reckford explored the harsh realities of unemployment in paradise with 'In the Beautiful Caribbean', while contributing to the *Empire Road* series and *Black Christmas*. The television plays tended to be two-dimensional, but at least authors were beginning to establish autonomy distinct from the previous importation of shows direct from Africa, the US, and occasionally from the Caribbean. Their potential was limited still to the expectations of established producers.

Trinidadian playwright, Matura, came to prominence in 1971 with *As Time Goes By*, presented at the Theatre Upstairs, and confirmed afterwards with *Play Mas* and then *Rum and Coca Cola*, staged at the Theatre Royal for three and five years respectively. Writers George Lamming and Andrew Salkey had established their careers in the United Kingdom before moving to the US where the tradition of black writing and theatre offered a wider scope. Their departure has not diminished the influence both men still have on the artistic talents in the black community in Britain.

By the mid-1970s, another Trinidadian writer, Samuel Selvon, emerged having written ten novels including 'A Brighter Sun' and 'The Lonely Londoners'. BBC television screened 'Home Sweet India' as part of the Commonwealth Season, while BBC radio had broadcast twelve of his plays, among them being - *Highway in the Sun, The Harvest in Wilderness, Milk In The Coffee* - set in England, and *Zeppi's Machine*. Radio has been generally a more effective medium for communicating the Caribbean experience in Britain, as well as the memories of the older generation in their formative years 'back home'.

Much drama originated from the community rather than from the established theatre. Jimi Rand produced, directed and acted in *No Cotton Pickers* at clubs, community halls and private venues, and later became artistic director of the Brixton Arts Theatre, the Lambeth Ensemble Theatre and the People's Art Company. Before him, Frank Cousins, who studied theatre administration at the London Polytechnic, founded the Dark and Light Theatre in South London, and took productions on tour to several European cities. He was principal member of The Black's cast.

The Black Theatre Co-operative produced *Welcome Home Jacko* and

One Rule by Matura. Though foremost, but not alone, these theatre groups matured in the 1970s and the early years of the next decade. The Keskidee Theatre in Islington, North London, hosted *Remembrance* by St. Lucian Nobel Prize laureate, Derek Walcott; *The Throne in an Autumn Room* by Lennox Brown, as well as Edgar White's *Lament for Rastafari*. *Mister Biko* and *Theresa* were probably the works best associated with the Temba Theatre Company at the time. At the dawn of the 1980s, awards for acting, writing and directing became popular.

Horace Ove, a Trinidadian who studied painting in Rome, became known initially through his direction of the film *Reggae* that focused on the Caribbean Music Festival at Wembley in 1970. From there he went on to make *Pressure* and *Hole in Babylon* (which looked at the Spaghetti House siege and in which T-Bone Wilson and Archie Schepp acted).

Pressure, in particular, is accredited with giving most poignant emphasis on the conflict from within and without in an oppressed community. Yet *Black Joy* and *The Harder They Come*, starring Jimmy Cliff, are the two black productions which overall had the greatest impact on the outside world.

Better known for his talents as a playwright, St. Kittian Caryl Phillips received acclaim for the novel 'The Final Passage' which was later adapted for television by Peter Hall and screened by Channel 4 in early 1997. Phillips is described as one of the finest and most important novelists of his generation. He and his parents left the island of St. Kitts when he was four months old. In his book, 'The European Tribe', he asserted that: "Black people have always been present in a Europe which has chosen either not to see us, or to judge us as an insignificant minority, or as a temporary, but dismissable mistake." Phillips is the recipient of numerous awards, including the Martin Luther King Memorial Prize. He is Professor of English at Amherst College, Massachusetts, US.

Guyanese Norman Beaton, who died in 1995, was a doyen of television entertainment in Britain. He brought a clean, sober and instructive approach to the performing arts, possibly because of his educational background and appreciation for Caribbean values. As a qualified teacher, he left his homeland to further his education in Britain. After finding difficulty with the education system, he turned to entertainment, mostly acting, beginning first with the Liverpool Poets group. He later acted in plays - the *Empire Road* - for instance. He even acted with English actor, the late Sir Laurence Olivier, on stage. Beaton featured in the films: *Black Joy* and the *Mighty*

Quinn, which included actor, Denzil Washington. At one time, the Guyanese starred with Bill Cosby, a leading American black entertainer. Yet it was the BBC television series, *Desmonds*, which portrayed Beaton's sheer brilliance - acting as Ambrose, the egotistical barber and family man. *Desmonds* was a big hit in Britain and elsewhere, and at one time in the early 1990s, had a viewing audience in excess of ten million. The support comprised fellow Guyanese, Carmen Munro and Ramjohn Holder of *Pork Pie* fame. Holder has promised to continue the standards of excellence that Beaton bequeathed.

Established prize-winning poet, James Berry, gleaned further honours with his collection of short stories for children - 'A Thief in the Night'. He was born in Jamaica but has lived in England for more than thirty years. His has worked for both radio and television. His best known publications include the selection of poems -'Lucy's Letter', 'Bluefoot Traveller' and 'Fractured Circles' - and for the prize-winning poem, 'Fantasy of an African Boy' in 1981.

Berry served on the Community Arts Committee of the Arts Council and the Literature Panel of the Greater London Arts. He received a Minority Rights Group Art Award for his writing in 1979. Towards the end of the 1980s, creative writing began to flourish in the black community and Berry was part of this rich tradition. He was to be followed by others Guyanese John Agard and Grace Nichols. Through his magical poetry and short stories, Agard publicised the richness of Caribbean folklore, while Nichols whose first books of poetry - 'I is a Long Memoried Woman' and 'The Fat Black Woman's Poems' - communicated the versatility of language and the creative power of the Caribbean artistic industry. Novelist Joan Riley is perhaps at the forefront of a new and more self-confident generation of women writers. Grenadian Jean Buffong's emerging literary talent should not be underestimated either.

Noteworthy, is the increasing number of loosely knit black writers' groups and workshops across England, most of which are led by black women. In the mid-1980s, the University of the West Indies cited the dominance of female writers in journalism and professional writing. Women are combining a blend of innovation and drive with enterprise unheard of prior to the last decade.

Distinctive in his 'Dub' style and appearance, Linton Kwesi Johnson, the editor of *Race Today*, is the poet with the largest audience through his public and television readings. His originality and consistency are unequalled in British literature today and are an inspiration to the black community. Desmond Rutherford summed up the inspiration which has fired many to poetry by dedicating his first book to 'sufferers' of the world, but he and others who wish to give expression to their feelings have had to publish their own works initially or give readings through the local government and adult education classes. Johnson's high profile, however, serves as an example that even a poet can succeed in his own age.

Another Guyanese, Wilson Harris, is a prolific writer. His first novel 'Palace of the Peacock' was published more than thirty years ago (it won him the Guyana Prize for Literature in 1987). Since then, he has published over a dozen novels and two books of literary criticism. Harris has held many positions in academia, including Associate Fellow at the Centre for Caribbean Studies, University of Warwick. Edgar Mithelolzer who left the then British Guiana to England in the first half of the 20th century is an outstanding literary artist. Before committing suicide several decades ago, he had published a series of illuminating publications - 'Swarthy Boy' and 'Corentyne Thunder' - which evoked pain, frustration and delight. They celebrated his authentic and indigenous form, derived from his own Amerindian-African Creole ancestry.

Grace Hallworth has put her childhood interest in folk-stories to good use in her books such as 'Listen to This Story', 'The Carnival Kite' and 'Mouth Open Story Jump Out'. As a director of the Bogle L'Ouverture publishing house, Jessica Huntley was responsible for opening the Walter Rodney Bookshop and for being the first to publish Linton Kwesi Johnson. Amryl Johnson, another Trinidadian, has published books of poems including 'Sequins for a Ragged Hem', 'Watchers and Seekers', and 'With a Poet's Eye'. She is a lecturer who has assisted pupils throughout Britain.

Trinidadian Faustin Charles, who has been residing in Britain for more than a generation, is an accomplished storyteller, novelist, poet and editor. He studied language and literature at the University of Kent. His readings are done in schools, the Commonwealth Institute and at annual Caribbean Day celebrations in London. He believes that oral traditions must be developed into a viable industry so that succeeding generations of African Caribbean heritage will be able to uphold strong values. In 1970 two of Charles' books of poetry were published. 'The Expatriate' is an account of the experiences of Caribbean people exiled in England.

While it has been accepted for some time in America that black people have contributed extensively to classical music - in composition, instrumentation and opera singing - the breadth of achievement in Britain is being understood and appreciated even more. Perhaps the more supposedly ethnocentric musical forms of reggae and calypso have distracted the attention of our neighbours from the fact that many middle-class black families like their young daughters to play the piano or take ballet (dancing) lessons. With our more recent colonial past we are probably more proficient in these Victorian traditions, unlike our white neighbours.

Samuel Coleridge-Taylor, the son of the famous surgeon, Daniel Hugh Taylor, became one of Britain's most popular composers. His choral composition, 'Hiawatha', is set listening for thousands of school children and their teachers, who are unaware that the composer was black. Coleridge-Taylor was not content to let his work alone represent his struggle for social equality. He became a founder member of the League of Coloured Peoples which was established in 1931 by Jamaican Dr. Harold Moody, who practised medicine in Camberwell, south London. Black singers have participated at the Glyndebourne Festival featuring the renditions of Coleridge-Taylor.

Rudolph Dunbar was a familiar conductor in England until he moved to the US where he later died. His flamboyant nephew, Guyanese Professor Ian Hall, came to public notice after performing in different artistic and musical roles. He attended Keble College, Oxford University and is reputed to be the first black musicologist to be trained there. Very intelligent and exceedingly talented, Hall spent some eighteen months in Ghana where he taught music to President Jerry Rawlings and other Africans. He has been director of music at several schools and an organist at concerts and recitals on radio and television. He is head of the Bloomsbury Society which was set up in 1971 to promote the arts in universities. Hall's compositions are usually dedicated to events or particular individuals. He is the author of published essays and verse. It is indeed a great pity that this musical genius is not popular with the mainstream media.

While researching this topic, I came across the names and addresses of the following African Caribbean theatrical, dance and artists groups in the 'Third World Impact' publication. I would like to quote a few to show the range and extent of our involvement in the literary arts industry in Britain. Nottingham: Black Velvet Dance Group, the Early Start Project and New Booker. Wolverhampton: L'Ouverture Theatre Trust and Ekome Arts. Bristol: Kutamba. Manchester: the London Youth Dance Theatre, Rainbow Art Group and the Sam Uriah Morris Society. London: Talawa Theatre Company and Phoenix Dance Company and various youth steelband groups.

Ray McLean, a powerfully built but supple man, taught many young dancers at the old Dance Centre in Floral Street, London, and showed himself to be a lithe entertainer at performances in Britain and abroad. Like many artists of his time, McLean is a Trinidadian. To be fair to his contemporaries, however, he was among instructors who created a lasting impression on students, most of whom later achieved excellence in their respective pursuits. Ray was in business long before the television *Fame* series caught up with reality.

Ivan Chin's band was an important feature of social events that became a classic. Chin served in the RAF at the end of the Second World War (1945-1947) and was a member of the West Indian Ex-Servicemen's Association. While working with his band at concerts throughout the European continent, he promoted Caribbean tourism and participated in meaningful community activities. He served as both secretary and treasurer of the Carib Housing Association, South London and was founder of the Guyana circle. Chin died in early 1997.

In July 1997, at the opening of Mahogany Limited, North-West London, junior minister of health, Paul Boateng, MP, reminded the audience of the vast contributions by Cy Grant to black British culture. Yet while Grant is famous for his talents as a calypsonian and an actor, it is often forgotten that he qualified as a barrister in 1951. He was co-founder and chairman of the Drum Arts Centre in 1974. Grenadian-born Alex Pascall, the broadcaster and former Chairman of the Notting Hill Carnival Arts Committee, is an accomplished drummer, singer and compere as well. He founded the Alex Pascall Singers and recorded the Anansi stories for broadcast. As an exponent in the performing arts, his understanding of the spectrum of African and Caribbean culture is beyond question. In 1974 he was invited to host the first black radio programme in Britain - 'Black Londoners' on Radio London. In early 1997, he was awarded an Order of the British Empire (OBE) for community development, including arts and culture.

Limbo dancing straddles the borderline between cultural art and popular entertainment. There are fewer competent professionals in this field than is often realised. Captain Fish and George Henry are two performers whose work is remembered best over a number of years. They had the ability to hold an audience, no matter how many times they appeared. Yet Henry and Fish gave much credit to fellow dancers for their success. Harry Girad who combined fire eating with (Eastern Caribbean) dance in the 1960s, returned to St. Lucia where he manages the Green Parrot.

Gloria Cameron played a vital role in preserving West Indian folk culture through the Caribbean Drama and Folk Group, which she formed in 1965. She produced several of her own shows, primarily in Lambeth, South London, and the group performed at charitable functions. Her involvement in community work included the formation of the West Indian Parent Action Group, and her membership on the boards of several drama, cultural and community relations groups.

After its decline in the 1970s, black women's theatre shifted emphasis from the exploration of serious drama to the treatment of art form as a commodity. Since 1982 however, the Theatre of Black Women (TOBW) was the vanguard of black women' theatre in Britain. That same year, playwright and drama director, Yvonne Brewster, OBE, became the first Black woman drama officer in the Arts Council of England (she formed the Talawa Theatre Company in 1985).

Bernadine Evaristo, Patricia Hilarie, Paulette Randall and Kadiji George are the founders of TOBW. After performing a series of plays, media interest in the organisation heightened in 1985. It has produced plays such as *Miss Quashi, The Tiger's Tail, The Cripple* and *The Children*. In spite of having its grant withdrawn in 1988, the TOBW is one of few groups responding to the needs of non-white women in the British artistic field.

Randall also worked as a director in a Repertory Theatre where she gained much experience. She directed several plays, including *24 Per Cent* (about the percentage of black women in British prisons) and *Headrock*. She has been a consultant director on a Lenny Henry tour and was, at one time, the sole producer of the popular television series, Desmonds.

Anxious to publicise the work of black women writers, Cheryl Robson founded the Aurora Metro Press in 1981. She became a recipient of the Pandora Award by Women in Publishing for her work in developing, publishing and promoting women writers in 1992. The Arts Council subsequently awarded her the Raymond Williams Publishing Prize for the success of seven plays by women - *Female Voices, Fighting Lives*.

It should be noted however, that Britain's burgeoning Black book trade had its genesis in the 1960s. Two decades on, the flow of black poetic talent grew stronger. Linton Kwesi Johnson, Grace Nichols, Benjamin Zephaniah, Valerie Bloom and Marsha Prescod, to name a few, often used 'nation language', groups of individual artists and writers to organise and develop their own publishing outlets.

Typical of this trend, was Akira Press, started by Desmond Johnson who came to London from Jamaica in 1988. A poet and publisher, he was inspired by existing projects - the Black Writers Workshop and the Black Ink Collective in Brixton. In eight months, Johnson sold a 5,000 copy edition of his poems, 'Deadly Ending Season', causing the West Indian Digest in 1985, to describe him as the poet and publisher 'who sells poetry like hot bread'.

Other new publishers included Yvonne Collymore's 'Arawdi', with books for Caribbean children, Lorna Miller's 'Inky Fingers', a collection of her own poetry, and Sandra Agar's 'Obatala Press' and 'Karnak House'.

In 1966, Trinidadian John LaRose founded New Beacon Books. His commitment to bring books to the community began literally with him taking them in a Marks & Spencer carrier bag to meetings. This developed into bookselling from his home until the business moved to Stroud Green Road in Finsbury Park, North London. A characteristic New Beacon title, 'Jamaican Airmen' by Martin Noble recognised the need for black people to record their history in Britain.

Bogle L'Ouverture Publications began two years later, with perhaps their most influential title, 'How Europe Underdeveloped Africa', by Guyanese historian, Dr Walter Rodney. This company also had its origin in the private home of founders - Jessica and Eric Huntley - after which they acquired premises in West Ealing (with the business renamed the Walter Rodney Bookshop after Rodney's assassination in 1980). Both Beacon and Bogle L'Ouverture were specialist outlets pioneering a tradition of community-based shops supplying black and Third World literature to readers in Britain, Africa, Asia, the Caribbean and North America.

The proliferation of independent black publishers at the time, reflected the mood among writers who were determined that their creative contribution must neither be ignored nor fall prey to changing fashion. A parallel necessity was also to include more black people into the organisational mainstream of printing and publishing.

More recently, black journalists from media institutions, frustrated by their inability to move up the success ladder and eager to enjoy autonomy, have established private companies ranging from management consultancy to training and public relations. One perfect example of this new development is the well known but graceful television presenter and journalist, Jacqui Harper, who is the owner of a rapidly expanding management training company. She is known for her work with the BBC, GMTV and Sky News. In the mid-1990s, Harper founded Crystal Media to make an impact on the world of communications training. Her clients include firms such as Abbey National, HSBC and Norwich Union.

Brenda Emanus who arrived in Britain form St. Lucia in the 1960s is a dynamic communications specialist. She freelances with various publications, mainly the Voice, and develops programme ideas for media production. She worked for the BBC on the black magazine programme Ebony, as a researcher and presenter, whilst presenting other programmes, including the Clothes Show and Travelogue for Channel 4.

Recently, Black women have combined their talents in an effort to provide a sustained quality of service to their community. The BiBi Crew was formed in 1991 and consisted of Joanne Campbell, Judith Jacob, Janet Kay (who has since left due to recording commitments), Suzette Llewellyn, Josephine Melville, Beverley Michaels and Suzanne Packer. Each actress has at least 10 years experience in theatre, television radio and film.

The company is dedicated to producing high quality new writing from an African Caribbean perspective and to introducing the black British experience to a larger cosmopolitan audience. Campbell is on the board of directors at the Theatre Royal, Stratford. Jacob starred in *Eastenders* and *The Real McKoy*. Kay has released an album entitled 'Love You Always' in Japan and her success in the record industry has meant she has had to leave the BiBi Crew. This group represents a new trend in the performing arts - where individuals from disparate backgrounds fuse their talents to realise each other's dreams.

Surprisingly, painters and other visual artists raised in the tropics of Africa and the Caribbean have retained their eye for colour, even after years in the fog and rain in Britain. Illustrations of the sun, the trees, and the water, seemed sharper in contrast to the actual first-hand experience. Few painters have depicted the tropical nights which in many ways are more impressive than the day, with the stars being overhead and seemingly so low that you could reach out and pick them. The heavenly bodies there are not obscured by the elements.

Ossie Murray, a Jamaican, who has spent years in the London boroughs adjoining Essex, is a specialist in defining the wooden landscape of his homeland. He has an eye for attractive ladies, and came to public attention some years ago for his lively portrait of Jennifer Hosten who, as Miss Grenada, won the Miss World Beauty contest in the early 1970s. Ossie also designed the pennants for the Commonwealth Sports Awards at Islington Town Hall. He has illustrated books and has taught through the now defunct ILEA and through his local borough administration.

Sidney Gellineau, who like Murray specialises in oil paintings, has been with Horace de Bourg and Errol Thorpe, amongst the best Trinidadian painters. They have exhibited at public and private functions, with encouragement from the Trinidad and Tobago High Commission. In spite of their years in Britain, West Indian painters maintain themes of their youthful days in the Caribbean. Yet black artists have not gained universal recognition or been adequately compensated financially, for their efforts, unlike their white counterparts. History has shown that only after death, the works of master-artists become best sellers.

De Bourg is unusual in that he favours water-colours and includes themes from Britain and location pictures from his visits to West Germany and the Netherlands. He has a lead role each year in the Civil Service art exhibition in Whitehall, and was chosen to paint a portrait of the former Conservative Prime Minister, Baroness Margaret Thatcher. Spectators of fashion shows and beauty contests on the North Sea ferries between Britain and Holland have seen his paintings on exhibition prior to the main event. De Bourg's works are displayed at various places in England on occasions.

Writing, painting and music are more difficult than most other artistic activities to quantify because apart from the few professionals involved, they are conducted at evening classes and schools throughout the United Kingdom as a pastime for enthusiastic amateurs. There is also a very fine line, if at all, between traditional art and the modern sciences, involving computer technology, in which our young men and women of today are excelling. Sir Christopher Wren observed for his memorial stone in St. Paul's Cathedral that the words should be "if you want a monument to me, look around." A visit to local libraries, art galleries and town halls would serve the same purpose in respect to enterprise in the arts.

Boyce Drake studied Fine Arts at the Gloucester College of Art and picture restoration in both Bristol and London. He commenced his first course in the mid-1950s and a quarter-of-a-century later, he won a scholarship to study picture restoration techniques at Stuttgart in West Germany. Boyce is a picture restorer and retailer of artists materials in Gloucester. He has chaired the city's International Friendship League.

There is no clear distinction between graffiti and mural paintings. The reason given often is that black youths in socially deprived areas, denied the usual artistic opportunities, brighten their lives by painting on available surfaces and stress their individuality in an otherwise anonymous environment through their highly personalised style. This argument could well be true. However, it is customary to paint pictures on walls of buildings in some parts of the Caribbean, and this manner of self-expression could be passed down from parents to children.

Some time ago, Alex Pascall wrote in the magazine, Saffron: "Black people have always had a medium of their own; that is, through talking to each other and passing the news along...The structure of the black media must go beyond what is put over the air or written on paper. Black people have a lot to talk about. I am a communicator - not a broadcaster. You must take any opportunity you can get to write for any paper or to carry out any research."

European art and literature have not always been as specialised as it seems today. Leonardo da Vinci, above all, and Michelangelo, mastered different fields of art and knowledge during the renaissance of classical culture. The black community may well be experiencing a similar revival. There are of course important differences in artistic themes. European artists have been willing to portray their pagan past before accepting Christianity. African Caribbean painting lacks a similar legacy in any depth, at least as far it concerns publicly exhibited works.

Much of the writings, especially poetry and drama of the 1980s, committed politically almost exclusively to the radical movements of socialism, and where applicable, to feminism. It is easy to understand therefore, the anger of the poor against what they see as inequalities in the society they live. The danger exists, however, that the anger may consume the art in a way that C.L.R. James, V.S. Naipaul and the writers of an earlier age managed to avoid, though it has to be admitted once again, that their social circumstances were considerably different.

Verna Wilkins of Grenada is bent on maintaining Caribbean literary excellence in Britain, with the establishment of Tamarind Limited, set up in 1987. Based in Camberley, Surrey, Tamarind is a highly respected publishing company dedicated to children's literature. When Wilkins first set up the business, she was advised that books with black children would not sell. One popular title, Dave and the Tooth Fairy, has sold 50,000 copies. It is now part of the national curriculum. The confident businesswoman believes that children learn from pictures before they learn to read.

The achievement of black people in sport, music and other popular art forms have worked against those who have the capacity to succeed in what society considers to be classic European arts. It is unlikely that a boy or girl from such a background would be taken seriously at school if he or she expressed an ambition to play the piano at concert recitals or to write a study on Jacobean drama. The ignorance of what our children are capable of achieving extends into other areas of scholarship or (for the purposes of this chapter) the intellectual enterprise.

Because the Caribbean territories and African countries have been a colonial football, West Indians have a particular knack for learning languages. From their chequered history, the inhabitants of some of the Eastern Caribbean sub-region, have grown up speaking French patois, as well as English, in the manner of traditional cultural value systems. Everyone engaged in commerce or administration needs to understand Dutch, French or Spanish to speak to his or her neighbours. There is a true story of a young lady, a model, who, while making a promotional trip to France, wondered how she could cope with her language. On her return to London, she told her agent: "There was no need to worry. Why didn't you tell me they spoke St. Lucian?"

Yet in spite of their learning, many of the most educated immigrants had to accept menial jobs when economic circumstances forced them to leave their homeland. It was not unusual to find a multi-lingual lathe operator, or a cleaner who could recite whole passages of Shakespeare, Keats or Yeats. Poets would contend that it gave them an even deeper appreciation or life. African Caribbean people are in the forefront of Bible study, and that does not exclude traditional (professional) theologians.

Undoubtedly, there is a reservoir of talent born of education and knowledge existing in the black community, but it is yet to find acceptance within the British society. The time is therefore, opportune for Britain to respond intelligently and positively to such infinite resources.

Hairdressing

The rudiments of Black British Enterprise are rooted in hairdressing. This profession has touched and influenced almost every aspect of early black business development, fuelling the growth of the multimillion pound industry which exists today. Unnoticed and unmentioned, the ethnic segment of the beauty industry has also produced the largest numbers of independent black business people in the UK.

I am reliably informed by those who should know, that the most reserved and secretive patron, once in his or her hairdressing chair, will often confide and pour out their innermost feelings to the person trusted with the care of their hair.

The unique attribute of a professional stylist is in her gift of creativity, that extra intrinsic something that satisfies the vanity of her patron in finding a wholesome fulfilment in a particular look.

It is a fact that women of all races are never satisfied with what they have. Black women with curly hair will go through endless processes to make it straight. White women with straight hair will go to the same extremes with perm lotions to make it curly.

Without doubt, it is the ladies who drive the beauty industry. Take a damsel into the woods and as she gets out, watch her movements and you will find that nine times out of ten she will always head straight for a mirror to examine her hair and make-up to see if they are still in tact!

In the early years of black emigrant arrivals, there were no salons or beauty parlours that catered for black hair, forcing them to engage in do it yourself mode.

Considering the unavailability of suitable beauty aids, emigrants were dependent on supplies from families or friends at home or from America. This obvious demand led directly to forging the rise of Dyke & Dryden Ltd which was founded in 1965 and stepped in to fill the gap in the market, later becoming Britain's best known black owned company.

Prior to the 1950s, there were virtually no black hairdressing salons. The trade was conducted in private home parlours, usually without planning permission. Patrons were obtained by referrals or on the grape vine. The business itself was in a way a meeting place for Caribbean nationals to exchange views on general issues relating to the Caribbean region. In some instances, visitors dropped by to either share or gain information about social events in the black community. Indeed, long before the term networking gained universal currency, black people had already perfected this art of social engineering.

The nature of the home working environment was such, that it restricted many of the pioneers from exhibiting their skills to the general public. A good hairdresser's services carried a premium and when one was found, patrons would travel from far to be sure of getting a good service.

As the demands of a more enlightened community became apparent at the beginning of the 1960s, black hairdressers sought to acquire premises suited to their needs.

This new businesslike approach now required taking into account operational costs and other overheads. Gradually, a breed of astute business women salon owners emerged to advance the industry. Most of them had prior experience in the informal home parlour or practical experience in the West Indies.

Recognition by the community of the business acumen displayed in pioneering the development of this remarkable service industry has been accorded to many of the major players who laid the foundation of the industry as we know it today.

These include some of the more prominent establishments that became household names such as Madame Rose of Harlesden, Dame Elizabeth of Hackney, Carmen England of Oxford Street, St Clairs of West End fame owned by George and Lorna St Clair, Aquarius of Finsbury Park and Splinters of Bond Street, are merely representatives of a much broader body of the profession.

Of a later era, companies like Supreme Hairdressing Salon emerged, fired with electric enthusiasm that forged a new breed of entrepreneurs. Supreme School of Hairdressing was not long in following, which had a remarkable impact on the industry.

Supreme was turning out hundreds of students which rapidly expanded the industry, with parlours opening in every neighbourhood where there was demand for hairdressing services.

As the business expanded beyond the immediate neighbourhood, salon owners had to find ways of bringing their services to a wider public. This development coincided with those of the embryonic Black Press. The publications in the 1960s included the English edition of the Jamaican Gleaner, the West Indian World and the West Indian Digest, and they were all supported by the hairdressing trade.

In return, these publications profiled the work of salon owners and improved their patronage and image.

This trend persisted into the 1980s, as publishers offered free point of sale advertorial which targeted the upwardly mobile and fashion conscious young ladies. Both the trade and the press benefited in that the emerging black sophisticated female patronage increased and at the same time the advertorials encouraged other businesses to follow the hairdressers example.

Many leading salons performed dual businesses, by becoming teaching institutions as well, which expanded the salon industry and employment prospects for many of their students.

Student graduation ceremonies became big social events in their annual calendars and did much in further promoting individual schools.

Admission to these events were by way of ticket sales and their popularity ensured the halls were always filled to capacity. These social events had a guaranteed knock-on effect on employment for a host of professionals, musicians, models, printers, caterers, photographers, designers, and uniformed commissionaires. A new generation of entrepreneurs emerged, promoting the black community culture in areas that they were well qualified to deliver.

Clever proprietors used these social events to good effect in cultivating good public relations with people with whom they do business. These included their bankers, prospective investors, suppliers, and prominent individuals in the society.

The success of these events was not lost on would be promoters in organising similar events, social organisations used the opportunity afforded by salon owners, to publicise their products and services to prospective customers. Graduation ceremonies presented by Madame Rose at the Porchester Hall in Paddington, at which the likes of the Honourable Mr. Marcus Lipton, the Member of Parliament for Brixton was a regular guest, together with a host of well known celebrities were highlights in the social calendar for thousands of supporters around London.

There was a typical West Indian flavour at these functions which included creative hairstyling competitions, fashion displays and music. Celebrated bands such as the Jamaican Jubilee Stompers and Eric Clarke and the Debonairs maintained a popular following for many years. These two well loved and competing bands were the most popular choices at graduation ceremonies and several other community functions.

Historically, hairstyles have been associated with the proclamation of youthful identity and protest. Angela Davis, the black American activist, popularised the "Afro Look" or the "Natural" as some prefer to call it. Manufacturers of the Afro wig, made to resemble black natural hair, made fortunes for Korean and Hong Kong companies who were the first to perfect the wig which became an accessory for any fashionable woman's wardrobe in the sixties and seventies.

It is said that everything goes around, and this could not be truer than in the case of the popularity of "Cane Rowing" or Plaiting, an African traditional hairstyle which is centuries old and in fashion today.

The popular hair fashion of the eighties that took the world by storm was the "*Wet Look*" or "*Curly Look*". The Curly Look Decade was a phenomenal success story for the companies that promoted the new innovation for people with afro hair. Carefree Curl, Sof'n Free and Leisure Curl, and TCB were market leaders in the US, with Super Curl in the UK.

What was amazing was the simplicity of the process itself, which entailed using a perm solution or gel to soften the hair and change its configuration by wrapping it onto rollers to arrive at the desired size of the curl.

The Executives of some of the manufacturing companies sported the new look, and branded it as the "*Executive Look*" which had an impact on the marketing of the product. This was particularly true of the two Ms, as they were affectionately known, McKenzie and Mc Bride of Sof'n Free.

The unisex nature of the product was worn not only by the ladies, but by men as well. The style's after care was a big plus for wearers. An afro pick and conditioning sprays were all that was needed to keep looking good, and what was more, the styles lasted longer and consequently were easier on the pocket.

In all this, hairdressers were the people that mattered, perfecting the look and creating variations, the wavy look, the dry look and the enhanced body perm.

Some hairdressers branched out into manufacturing. George and Lorna St Clair of St Clair's were astute business people and quite correctly capitalised on the reputation they had built up for quality work and service and launched their own product line under the brand name of St Clairs.

The St Clairs were role models for the young, starting out with a small premises in Praed Street in Paddington, and soon after moved to two new sites at Marble Arch and Sheperds Bush, attracting the middle class clients.

They were also well known for their community activities and for sponsoring successful Steel Bands at the annual Notting Hill Carnival.

In an interview with the first edition of West Indians in Great Britain 1973/74, Lorna had this to say. *"I would have liked to see greater co-operation and support amongst West Indians to enable us to build a strong and viable foundation."* Her husband felt that lack of confidence was a major factor hindering West Indians from succeeding in business.

Another hairdresser, Enoch Williams of Glamourland, also branched out into manufacturing with products of his own under the brand name of Sahara. This product line has been well received in the conditioning segment of the market.

Young hairdressers, male and female, recognised that their hairdressing skills provided an outlet for expressing a common identity with the cultures of the diaspora, and moved to countries where their skills were needed. Some went to North America while others went to Africa.

The importance of the Caribbean and Afro Hair Society should not be underestimated. It has played a major role in cultivating professional standards for its members, and further played a key role in keeping the use of professional products out of the hands of the general public.

The US has been in the forefront of new techniques in the industry and salons would travel to the annual Bronner Brothers exhibition in Atlanta in large numbers from many parts of the world, where new products and systems are always on show. It must be said however that black British stylists working in the States always cut an envious dash with their presentations and are regularly sought after.

Two magazines dedicated to the industry, Black Beauty Professional and Black Beauty & Hair, provide technical and professional advice, and carry high quality photographs of hairstyles, together with contributions on other aspects of fashions, hints on colouring, advice on careers in beauty, tips on skin and health care, as well as a directory of salons throughout the country too numerous to mention. An entire industry has developed from popular hairdressers and has been fuelled particularly by the introduction of a wide range of beauty products, many of which are imported from the US.

The American hair and beauty products industry is interesting and important to the African Caribbean youth in Britain, not merely because of common cultural and physical characteristics.

The US experience shows that black people can build industries, and indeed create fortunes from humble beginnings. Madame C.J. Walker, who was born as Sara Williams in St. Louis, Missouri, was the first black woman to become a millionaire by being successful in the cosmetic industry and was an example for others to follow. It was reported that it was after meeting with lawyers F.F. Ransom and Robert Lee Brokenburr in 1910, that Walker was given the impetus to start her own business and make a fortune.

Her initiative was followed by both Sara Spencer Washington and Madame Molly Malone, in introducing Apex and Poro Beauty products respectively. By the 1930s and 1940s, Philadelphia was a business centre with a wide range of black-owned companies in the beauty industry.

New Jersey and New York followed the example of Philadelphia black businesses to the extent that the Black Eastern Domestic Manufacturing Association was set up in the early 1950s to promote beauty products in other areas of the US.

The founding of Johnson Products company by George E. Johnson in 1954, with the introduction of his Ultra Sheen relaxing system, could be cited as the start of the age when owners of black beauty products came on stream in a big way. Johnson's Products was the first black owned company to be quoted on the New York stock exchange and revolutionised the processing of black hair.

The leadership and technical expertise was a huge leap forward for hairdressing and black women the world over sang Johnson's praises.

In Britain, Dyke and Dryden was the first to produce products on the home front and here again it was hairdressers who spearheaded the testing and promotional activities that made the breakthrough possible. Mrs Joan Sam of Supreme School of Hair Design, in particular, has to be credited for her role in this area.

The Afro Hair and Beauty Exhibition founded in 1982 by Dyke & Dryden is the premier market place for the industry and its continuing success is also driven by hairdressing.

From the selection of models for the all important hair product demonstrations and competitions, the hairdressers' skills had to be in the forefront of preparation and delivery of the end products for public acceptance.

While a quality product will in the end always sell itself, it is its presentation that will capture the attention of the hordes of attendees at a product launch against competitive brands.

The Americans are past masters in making presentations of what is described as the *"Total Look"*, hence the common currency used in presentations and it is referred to as the "SHOW".

To some extent the hairdressing industry depends on presentation and imagery. Magazines for instance, enhance trends and project images captured skilfully by professional photographers. Angus Thompson has been a leading figure in this field.

The Afro Hair and Beauty Event is now institutionalised, attracting thousands of exhibitors and visitors from many parts of the world. It is mentioned annually in the British Tourist Board's " *What to see in Britain.*"

Black British Hairdressers must take a large part of the credit for delivering this edifice of Black Enterprise. I recall a quote from a speech I made in 1985 at the Exhibition. " *It is fitting that we arrived at the Wembley Conference Centre in our 20th anniversary year, to mount the biggest Black exhibition ever held in Europe for our industry. This represents an unmistakable contribution which we, as a community, can all be justly proud of.*"

That year, the programme offered, three days of pleasurable business, full of fun and enjoyment. Competitions filled with creativity included acts such as the *"Battle of the Barbers"*, where the barber sculpted wild and wacky designs, hairstylists demonstrated their creativeness for day or evening styles in the *"Battle of the Divas"*, while the young students engaged in free styling competitions which enabled them to exhibit their originality. The advanced professional stylist entered the *"Avante Garde Hair Competition"* extravaganza which gave free reign to their imagination.

Regular exhibitors who have supported this event over the years, include Carsons Products Co., Summit Labs, Lustrasilk, D-Drum Hair Products , Hollywood Curl, Johnson Products Co. Ltd., Keystone Laboratories Inc., Luster Products , Palmers, Pro-Line Ltd., Revlon, Sheernoir, Soft Sheen Products Inc., and the TCB Division of the Alberto Culver Company Ltd, and M&M Products, a formidable array of American corporations.

The British contingent is always there supporting the home engine of the industry. An important fact that must always be taken into account is that the hairdressing industry was the seed bed for many new business start-ups.

Black enterprise development in Britain has, as we have seen, had its roots in hairdressing in no small measure. It is virtually impossible to document the enormous contributions of other pioneers in the hair and beauty business.

One thing for sure that the foregoing demonstrates, is that there is no lack of enterprise in the black community, contrary the perception held by some financial institutions who hold the keys to the community's advancement in playing its part in the economic life of the nation.

The twin sister to hair fashions are the clothes shows that go hand in hand, and designers who made the events sparkle include the very gifted designer and co-ordinator, Karen Hamilton .

Her boutique included the work of designers, Caroline Arewa, Jean Daley, Cecile Jeffreys, Lorna Parkinson, Omar Zahir, Sylvia McIntosh, Verna Pinnock and Paul Hamilton, whose work complemented the outstanding shows of the time.

The late Carmen England is credited as the first black woman in England to have established a hairdressing salon in fashionable Mayfair in 1948. She studied hair and beauty culture in London, New York and Paris. She chaired the West Indian Carnival Queen Committee from 1959 to 1962 and received numerous awards.

In a magazine interview, a representative of Jades of Mayfair said that variation in style was a competing factor in contemporary fashions: There are often stronger trends in black hair because it does not grow as quickly as European hair. It also lacks movement which is where European hair has an advantage over us. Afro hair is solid and I am waiting for the day when a new product is developed so that we can make hair more moveable and pliable.

That comment is now dated and included merely to show how technology in dealing with black hair has moved on.

Perhaps one of the more exciting developments in the hairdressing industry is the movement of black hairdressers carving out a share in the European segment of the market.

Acquisition of white owned salons by black salon operators caused apprehension by the clientele of the previous owners. This concern was soon swept aside as the new owners quickly demonstrated by the service they provided that their fears were unfounded.

Thus, hairdressing which was once the yardstick for cultural differences, soon transcended attitudes which were more in the mind rather than for real.

Black hairdressing history is secure in the part it has played in the early development of Black Enterprise in Britain.

Health & Community Care

While the investment of black human capital pervades the whole national social structure, there is nowhere it is possibly more pronounced than in the Health Service.

African Caribbean people are so closely identified with the Health Service that a young lady visiting a town or village not acquainted with black people will assume that she is a nurse, a nursing auxiliary or a maid unless informed otherwise. Black actresses gained prominence through televised roles as nurses on television or on stage. Elizabeth Adare and Jumoke Dabayo are among this group. The last four decades of the past century saw successive British Governments carry out recruitment drives in the West Indies for Health Service personnel, as the native population were reluctant to take up these important but undervalued roles.

For some time, nurses dominated theatrical shows and beauty contests as they tried to leave a profession which they were encouraged to work in as a matter of course - out of financial necessity. Beautician Della Finch and pin-up model, Lucienne Camille were nurses for years. Sandie Parkes won the Miss Westindian title in 1979 and gave up modelling to concentrate on a nursing career. It was clear that the trend had been reversed and that younger women particularly, considered nursing as a career rather than being confined to some uninspiring career prospect.

For decades, matrons, nurses and doctors managed hospitals and related health institutions, while health visitors and administrative personnel looked after the general medical needs of the public.

It took time for early immigrants, while employed in great numbers in hospitals around the country, to be promoted to senior positions of authority comparable with their working knowledge, qualifications and ability. This situation however, changed, but not without first overcoming many of the racial barriers that worked against them.

It is therefore immensely heartening to see women of colour achieving and gaining competitive positions of authority richly deserved. Examples of this situation are evidenced by the position of Dame Carlene Davis, Director of Nursing, Royal College of Midwives, and the first Jamaican to hold this office.

The late Lord Pitt achieved eminence in various fields of endeavour (which is often forgotten) prior to his ennoblement when he was known as

Dr. David Pitt. He left his birthplace Grenada to study medicine at Edinburgh University in Scotland, a year before the outbreak of the last war. After a few years in Trinidad, he returned in 1947 and continued to work as a general practitioner. Throughout his medical profession he became actively involved in political and social affairs. He served as President of the British Medical Association and chaired the former Greater London Council. His peerage was conferred on him in 1975.

There is an interesting linkage that runs through the first generation of immigrants in medicine. Doctors had probably more contacts with a wider cross-section of the community, and built relationships with established institutions and professional bodies.

Large numbers of African and West Indian students studied medicine and practiced in various areas of the profession. Through this mechanism, they influenced change as we have seen in the case of Lord Pitt.

Dr. Victor Page, a Jamaican dental surgeon, was a prominent member of the community in South East London, where he also served as a Justice of the Peace. In addition, as Chairman of the Governors of the West Indian Students Centre, he did much in changing public perception of the African Caribbean community.

Physiotherapist, Ally Nazeer, arrived in Britain in the early 1950s and studied at the University of London Institute. He was appointed a Justice of the Peace. He was founder president of the Waltham Forest Islamic Association and founder member of that borough's Community Relations Council.

Owen Eversley, a chiropodist, physiotherapist, and osteopath lived and practised in South-east London. He was born in Barbados and came to England in the 1950s. He was a regular spokesman for his compatriots on radio and through the Barbados Overseas Community and Friends Association. He had a keen interest in cricket and social welfare and later became Barbados High Commissioner to London.

Most Caribbean women are blessed with an innate gift of tender loving care and no doubt it is this God given attribute that has drawn them to the nursing profession in increasing numbers.

A fact, which needs to be noted, is that they refuse to allow racist abuse and prejudice by patients to stand in the way of their professionalism. They see these as issues to be addressed by example.

The kind of care and dedication I refer to might be best illustrated by the legendary Mary Seacole in the way she used her skills in combating the Jamaican cholera epidemic of 1850, and travelling extensively in England, the Greater Antillies, the Bahamas and Central America offering care and attention to those who needed it. In 1853, she volunteered her help to soldiers fighting in the Crimean war, and with no encouragement and help from the military or medical authorities, she made her own arrangements and travelled to the battle field and saved the lives of soldiers suffering from yellow fever.

Haringey's first Black female Mayor, Erline Prescott, who left office in 1995, is both a health stalwart and community leader. Hers is the story of a woman who came from relative political obscurity in 1988 when she joined the Labour Party, to become the First Citizen in her borough in 1994. In 1959 she left Trinidad to advance her education. After leaving school, she worked in advertising, before enrolling at the Chelsea School of Chiropody. From 1969, she worked as a chiropodist with the National Health Service, serving communities and hospitals across London.

Ann Campbell qualified as a nurse and was elevated to matron. Her qualifications in administration complimented her position in the hospital's hierarchy.

The link between social work and the community is very deep seated. Pearl Giwra, qualified as a nurse and her propensity to community care led her to becoming a member of the Brixton Neighbourhood Community Association.

In an effort to pursue what was her first love, she gave up nursing to enter full-time community work. She was concerned about the welfare of retired West Indians.

Mildred Pemberton, also a qualified nurse from St Kitts, like Pearl Giwra also gave up nursing for charitable work and eventually opened a nursing agency to help the community.

Like-minded Jamaican nurse Iris Skeete trained in Bristol and settled for working with youth and social organisations. Her expressed underlying religious conviction, led to participation in community welfare work: " I love the Lord Jesus Christ, I worship with the Assemblies of God through-out Great Britain and Ireland and find it quite rewarding. "(first edition of West Indians in Britain).

Her compatriot, Thelma Lewis, a medical laboratory technician, was a founder member and secretary of the Cheshire Home (UK Working Committee), member of WISC, and the British Caribbean Association.

The late Cliff Lynch, a dental technician, is best known for his public relations work at WISC. He arrived in Britain more than forty years ago after studying in the US, and was encouraged to become involved in public affairs after the murder of Kelso Cochrane in Kensington during the Notting Hill riot of 1958. Lynch was a frequent contributor at the Speaker's Corner at Hyde Park in West London.

Fellow Jamaican, Clement Miller, himself a dental ceramist, was succeeded by his two sons. Miller possessed another well-known attribute - he was a learned theologian.

Yet another early Jamaican, Milton Russell, was also an accomplished dental technician with a City & Guilds diploma. He enjoyed carpentry, gardening, angling and generally had a passion for leisure. He was a member of the Hertfordshire and Leigh-on-Sea Amateur Angling Club.

Edward Williams came from Montserrat and worked as a pharmacist, after living in the US. He attended Portsmouth College of Technology. He encouraged West Indian parents to take a keener interest in their children's education and urged the younger generation to take advantage of education facilities.

Guyanese Carmen Steele, a qualified nurse, became a ward sister by the early 1970s. She felt that improvements were necessary for nursing students using recreational facilities and worked hard to implement them, which afforded her immense satisfaction.

In recent times, British doctors born to West Indian families are making their presence felt on the Health Service. Dr. Petular Caesar of Dominican parents graduated from the University of Aston and obtained her PhD in artificial liver support and related systems. Thereafter, she worked on a research project in foetal lung disorders at Southampton General Hospital.

Dr. Winston Martin 36, of Jamaican parents, is currently one of youngest and most brilliant heart surgeons in the country today. After leaving medical school Dr. Martin worked in several hospitals specialising in surgery. After a spell in Switzerland, he returned to England as a specialist consultant in cardiology.

West Indian doctors of an earlier era, have had a significant impact on London and the late Victorian and Edwardian age. Theophilus Scholes, a Jamaican, studied medicine at Edinburgh University in the 1880s, half-a-century before Dr. Pitt followed suit, and undertook missionary work in Nigeria and Zaire. He returned to England at the turn of the century and wrote several books, which had much influence on the Pan-African movement.

His missionary experience shaped his views on colonialism, and distinguished African and Caribbean visitors and residents in Britain sought his audience.

Sierra Leonian-born Daniel Hugh Taylor, the father of composer Samuel Coleridge-Taylor, decided to settle in Britain in the 1870s, becoming a qualified member of the Royal College of Surgeons and a Licentiate of Physicians. He practised as an assistant to a doctor in Croydon, after whose death he returned to Africa. Taylor found that the prejudice then present in society prevented him from practising successfully in his own unique way.

For many who believe in posterity, the African medical practitioner will be remembered more as the father of a famous son rather than for his own professional skills.

Trinidadian Dr. John Alcindor came to Britain in 1893 and studied at Edinburgh University for six years. After graduating he became an anaesthetist at Paddington Infirmary, West London. Over the next decade he held a number of positions and wrote on influenza, cancer and tuberculosis and established his own practice on the Harrow Road. Alcindor was a keen cricketer and a Roman Catholic, as well as a friend of Samuel Coleridge-Taylor and his family. He was head of the African Progress Union of London and in 1921, opened the Pan-African Congress by advocating that the battle for black rights should be fought with dignity and discretion.

Three years later Alcindor died, and an obituary in *West Africa* read "Dr. Alcindor was perhaps the best-known practitioner in London amongst African people, though his professional skill was by no means limited to them." He had worked for the Red Cross for the last seven years of his life. He was one of Paddington's four medical officers under the Poor Law Scheme.

James Jackson Brown was a Jamaican who studied in Canada before commencing studies at the London Hospital in 1905. After passing his final examinations nine years later, he settled down to family life. His practice was located in Hackney, East London, where he treated many patients who suffered from venereal diseases. It was said that he found his race too embroiled in idle gossip and gave them a wide berth. This remark, it is said, caused him to be considered a mystery man in the neighbourhood.

He was reputed however, to have had a large circle of social friends in the African and Caribbean community.

Dr. Harold Moody, a Jamaican, was prominent in the League of Coloured Peoples from its inception in 1931 until his death sixteen years later. He and Brown, who died in the early 1950s, were present during the bombing of the Second World War. Brown is credited with restoring the health of Jamaican lawyer 'Jags' Smith and was succeeded in his practice by Barbadian Dr. Colin Franklin.

Another Barbadian, Cedric Clarke, established his own extensive practice in South London in the 1930s.

As with nurses it is impossible to name or track the thousands of trained persons in Britain. Some, as we have seen, have stayed and made valuable contributions to the Health Service, while others have returned to their own countries where their services were needed.

Over the last 50 years two health hazards peculiar to the blacks have dogged the community. Sickle-Cell Anaemia and the high incidence of mental illness. In the case of the former condition several community attempts have been on-going in an effort to find a solution for sufferers.

Neville Clare, a Sickle cell sufferer, founded the Organisation for Sickle Cell Research (OSCAR) in 1975 and became manager of the project. Mr. Clare is a member of the Haringey Community Health Council and Disablement Association, and largely due to his active concern with others, OSCAR has become possibly the best-known acronym in the Afro Caribbean community. Organisational, medical and celebrity support is ongoing to keep the condition in the public eye.

Elizabeth Aninonwu is Head of the Brent Sickle Cell and Thalassemia Centre in North London. Previously, she worked as a health visitor and a tutor in the area . She received a CRE Bursary, a Health Service Association Scholarship and a King's College Fund Scholarship to help in furthering her work in seeking to obtain greater recognition for the sufferers of Sickle Cell and Thalassemia.

The community owes a debt of gratitude to people like Patricia Martin-Del-Burgo, a psychiatric nursing sister, who was awarded a prize for nursing and her dedication to care.

Laris Fisher came to Britain from Jamaica over twenty years ago. She was trained in general nursing at the Ipswich and East Suffolk General Hospital and studied midwifery and health visitor education. Ms. Fischer became Britain's first full-time Sickle Cell social worker in 1985.

Pansy Jeffrey's experience shows the link between health and dealing with the problems of contemporary life. She was trained as a nurse and later became a health visitor and health education specialist in Brent. Ms Jeffrey is organiser of the community service of the Citizens Advice Bureau in Kensington, and a founder member of the Pepper Pot Club for elderly West Indians. Ms Jeffrey was included in the Queen's Jubilee Honours in 1977.

Venisawelah Olafisoye came to England from Barbados over thirty years ago, and qualified as a State Registered Nurse (SRN) within two years. Six years on, she received the Clifford Morrison Award for proficiency in surgery.

For more than a generation, the NHS has drawn on a huge pool of cheap labour in nursing and auxiliary labour from the Caribbean, West Africa, and the Indian sub continent.

It is patently impossible to quantify the contribution made to the Health Service and Community Care by black people. Clearly the service can ill afford to function without them. We should not underestimate however, the selfless commitment, dedication and loyalty to the human cause that many of us have and still are demonstrating in Britain.

These sterling qualities cannot be ignored or lost on a dependant public.

The foregoing does not claim to give a full account of the Caribbean's contribution, but merely serves to draw attention to the facts of its long and continued service to the Health Service.

The Late Mrs Daphne Wade who gave her life in serving the Health Service

Beauty Contests & Fashion

Our contribution to beauty and fashion in the United Kingdom is unquestionable, if not unparalleled. Bruce Oldfield is probably the country's best-known designer at this time, though he is one of many to impact on the trade. An Englishwoman remarked that we Caribbean people brought colour to what had been a very dreary and grey picture. Little wonder British fashion can hold its own anywhere else in the world.

Admittedly England was still suffering from the economic and psychological effects of the Second World War when West Indians began to arrive here in significant numbers. Nevertheless (newsreel) films of the pioneers on the Empire Windrush were conspicuous by their suits and hats, being characteristically different from the lacklustre garb of the resident population. There are two specific sectors in which our influence became apparent during the period of immigration.

More West Indian women turned to sewing at a professional level than other women in various communities. It was a combination of tradition and economics when shop-clothes were too expensive for their modest income. Women repaired clothes for their own families and once proven competent, extended their services. This cottage industry is yet to be credited for its creativity and enterprise spirit, not to mention being included in the local economic indexation system.

The indigenous English considered a fashionably dressed man, especially if his clothes were ostentatious, as akin to a sissy. This label was tagged on foreigners, particularly Italians, and with rebellious minorities such as the Teddy Boys. Without losing our masculinity we West Indian men showed beauty, grace and poise in our dress and general demeanour. Today, teenagers and adolescents are very fashion-conscious, as the trendy outfits testify. Yet, it is we who have really introduced that sense of cultural uniqueness in the ethnic melting pot of British society.

In addition, African and West Indian politicians, as well as other prominent persons in society, instituted their own formal dress code. The bush jacket, the Nehru-type jacket and traditional costumes are integral to the diplomatic and social fashion-conscious paraphernalia. Few of us are involved directly but people bounded by informality and formality usually imitate such attitudes and practices with respect to fashion. Of course, it must be emphasised that such values help to celebrate the beauty of the human form.

European audiences have been acquainted with African fashions for a long time. They have formed an important part of the chic salon shows in Paris and Milan for a generation. Black models for example, could earn a decent living in West Germany and Switzerland before a full-time career was possible in Britain. France responded favourably to the flamboyant Josephine Baker from the inter-war years. Exotic styles were piquant and an essential element to quality fashion displays.

The European market was quick to accept the most humble of excellent (fashion) designs, unlike music or other aspects of our culture. Perhaps by staging our community fashion shows, and including American trends, we have not been able to attract the high profile in the export sector that our designers have deserved or could have obtained. Thankfully all of that is changing, now that everyone is more aware of the potential.

However, as a community, we need to intensify the promotion of the artistic industry, which has tremendous potential. Something similar has happened in swimming.West Indians are raised in the water but the competitive aspect of the sport is missing. Indeed, I can't think of any African-Caribbean representative in the British swimming team. Young people cite fashion as being their main interest when interviewed by newspapers and magazines. Root magazine is the sole publication that has given a fair amount of coverage on fashion, though this is often imitative rather than creative.

Sheila Brown is one of few West Indian writers in Britain who specialises in fashion through her articles in the Gleaner, the West Indian World and several Nigerian magazines. In the early 1980s, publications from West Africa, including *Happy Home, Super Woman* and *Africa Woman*, achieved recognition until their circulation in Britain was cut back in the wake of the events of late 1982. Through the Gleaner, Herma Diaz has offered a consistent view of the international fashion trade.

While African and Caribbean people dominate the hair and beauty products industry, the fashion trade is still treated as entertainment. This limits designers and manufacturers from maximising opportunities for growth and expansion. Since the beginning of the 1990s, several beauty consultants have hit the market, but few have intelligently studied the market and the general business environment. There is also a lack of quality information on African-Caribbean fashion designers and manufacturers, as well as distributors.

The use of photography to capture fashion imagery is a hallmark of

West Indian culture, although there are not many specialists in fashion or modelling photography among us, such as the likes of David Bailey. The image that we present is largely influenced by the observation or views of others. That does not mean that West Indians haven't mastered the art of international photography; far from that, we have expertise in other fields as well. Bill Patterson, a photo journalist, is a typical example of the person I have in mind - and, of course, there is Angus Thompson and Carl Gabriel.

What is the essence of Caribbean fashion? It is acknowledged that West Indian young women share the same flair as the French because of the ties which bind our colonial heritage with distinctive styles, despite territorial and cultural variations. Like the rhythms of the Caribbean region, fashion manifests a profound sense of cultural identity.

Colonial powers like France and Spain complemented the Caribbean cultural fabric like others in the Americas. The Dutch, noted more for their commercial interests than their gaiety, however, left their only legacy in the artistry of Van Gough. In the imperial age, it was the British influence on culture that was predominantly utilitarian. Thus Caribbean culture remains fertile and is unique to existing cultures in other traditional societies.

The dynamics of the African contribution emerged from an entirely different cultural experience because communities and families were divided and suppressed. African society developed heterogeneously due to a pervasive European influence. On the other hand, a substantial Asian input dominates Guyana, Trinidad and the eastern Caribbean.

But is hasn't stopped there. West Indian designers have introduced innovations. Cindy Breakspeare, the former Miss World, has advocated the greater use of shells for design which are plentiful in the islands. The difficulty in developing a distinctive black British fashion identity is due to the changing trends in emphasis. There is an over-reliance on either African, American or European models rather than on the unique characteristics of West Indian culture.

The American society has influenced new fashions throughout the world. A sophisticated and widely supported media network depicting that country's obsession with affluence reinforces this. Its military might is even advertised with the use of black GIs returning from the war. This Western trend existed long before Motown stars, such as the Temptations and Four Tops, were in the vanguard of male fashion in the US, not forgetting the original Jackson Five musical group (before they broke up with Michael Jackson, now King of Pop, creating more and more stunning breakthroughs in both the performing arts and the glamour business in a white-controlled market).

The recent appeal for male fashion contests has done little more for modelling than their female counterparts. There is a difference of opinion as to whether the winner should be cool, sophisticated and beautiful, or macho and muscular. The participants in these charades are not valued as individuals - titleholders are not remembered in the manner of beauty queens - and in spite of their instant popularity, no male model has gained public recognition. The position could change in the next decade.

Nevertheless, men have played an instrumental role in developing fashion consciousness. Al Shelly is a good example in this regard. He was one of the West Indian dancers to have appeared on television in the mid-1960s, and who taught another generation of male and female models at a well-known school in Oxford Street. In the last twenty-five years, Al acquired incomparable experience in aspects of modelling, the anonymous but highly prized catalogue work, television and the theatre.

Shakira Baksh, the former Miss Guyana Beauty Queen, is a credit to all West Indians in Britain. She enjoys immense popularity in spite of her inability to capture the Miss World title in 1967 - though she appeared to be the winner the previous year. As a self-made celebrity, she cuts an excellent public figure as the wife of British film star, Michael Caine. Quite interestingly, she has maintained her distinctive cultural identity and not bowed to the distractions and temptations of Hollywood fame.

The younger group of fashion models today have to contend with the sublime to the ridiculous from a highly sensational media, craving for so-called 'juicy' stories. Despite setbacks in her career, British-born black model supremo, Naomi Campbell, has reinforced the truism - that Black Culture sets the trends and dominates the markets in the world of fashion and music. In an editorial comment in the Weekly Journal on April 16, 1997, Campbell spoke of the injustices meted out to black female models by white editors. The Journal reported that the fashion world *"undervalued and undermined black models"*. Some argue that it was unfortunate that Campbell, who is also a self-made entrepreneur, waited until her career was finally established before she took issue with a highly competitive and often hostile industry of fame and glory.

The biased critical judgment may seem to be tortuous arising from the early localised beauty shows providing cheap entertainment for an economically depressed community, to the world of high fashion. Yet every woman who appears in public wishes to identify with that glamorous world. And why shouldn't she! Fashion itself is about beauty and inspiration. Our black business community, as evidenced from current economic regeneration programmes in Britain, should seize upon the growing recognition of the need to develop cultural industries. African-Caribbean people must thus be proud when designs and other fashion products are publicised depicting the artistry and cultural heritage of the region.

With commercial stakes mounting and a host of activities involved, it is difficult to gauge public attitude to beauty contests, which themselves have changed considerably. In the context of the Caribbean community, beauty contests and hair-styling graduations at public halls are germane to the development of fashion and entertainment industries in Britain. Even community-minded organisations such as the West Indian Standing Conference, the West Indian League, the Brockley International Friendship Association and the Willesden Unity Association, considered annual beauty contests essential to their programme of activities.

The competition satisfied the requirements of a community lacking finance and alternative outlets. Contestants required no equipment other than themselves, and for an evening, they left the drudgery of routine tasks to take centre stage. "It gave me a chance to be somebody", is the candid view of ambitious young ladies for whom opportunities to win awards were rare. The early participants were the brightest of their generation.

Difficulties aside, African-Caribbean communities were well positioned to exploit these opportunities because their situation connected them to others who taught skills, and their social milieu provided attachments to a prospective source of labour.

Promoters gained solid support from families and friends. Success was thus guaranteed and links were strengthened in the locality. A distinct feature of West Indian contests is the large percentage of women who attend to cheer on their relatives, friends or colleagues. Unattached men, for the most part, only attend to 'eye up' participants.

These cultural displays have an added advantage for the black community business talents. For the future businesswomen, prospective models, singers and dancers, it is a confidence-building exercise having to appear in public. Some women, especially poorly paid nurses working under unfavourable conditions, used this exposure to improve their lot. However only few, if any, did realise their ambitions in this new-found career. The beneficiaries were the local community and private individuals who prepared models and other contestants for competition.

Thus a whole new industry was spawned for dressmakers, designers, hair stylists and beauticians. Entertainers, journalists, photographers and caterers welcomed the chance to perfect their skills. Everyone engaged in the industry found a forum to discuss, negotiate and arrange deals. Photographs of beautiful young women at well-attended promotions attracted press attention and soon commercial sponsors appreciated their value.

The Jamaican Overseas Families and Friends Association (JOFFA), inspired by L.E. Campbell travel agency, brought the local strands together in a nationally recognised competition in 1966. They introduced a pattern of promotion, which became a standard-bearer for all parties involved in promoting beauty contests and fashion shows. The quality of contestants nevertheless determined the strength of the early Miss JOFFA shows.

Nicola Lodge was the first title-holder. Her comprehensive contribution to the industry is unequalled. Nikki was already a leading model of that time, along with Sylvana Henriques, Beryl Cunningham and Sherry Joseph, but during her reign she showed ability as an administrator and in public relations. Afterwards Miss Lodge returned to Jamaica and several years later, she returned to Britain as the chaperone of her homeland's representative in the Miss World competition.

Dyke & Dryden Ltd was another leading commercial enterprise with a respected beauty title in the late 1960s. The company was to some extent a victim of its own success. The Beauty pageant was a significant marketing platform in the development of the company's brands, the growth of which became the company's core activity with greater demand on management time. By the turn of the decade, Dyke & Dryden withdrew, at a time when also the nature of the industry itself changed from its original conception.

There were other promoters in the formative years. Hugh Scotland presented highly publicised shows at the Lyceum, but he left no tradition when he migrated to the US. The Barbadians and Guyanese were in the forefront in arranging specific titles for territorial communities. Newspaper reports of the winner's prize trip to the Caribbean provided the link between compatriots on either side of the Atlantic. This characteristic would remain even when most other aspects of the industry were discredited.

The decline occurred suddenly in the early 1970s. There were many reasons for this. Essentially, the independent promoters who took over

Miss JOFFA launched titles of their own such as Miss Black and Beautiful. The shows were organised as a commercial venture and this move affected the social function - a service, to which the community had grown accustomed. By reducing the number of participants and some of the glamour, the promoters in effect destroyed a potentially viable enterprise built on the rich traditions of the black community.

The next generation of promoters - Sammy Jay Holder, Rafael Albert and Chris Francis - were all journalists or photo-journalists. They had reported on the major competitions of the 1960s and were eager to recreate that environment. The world of the late 1970s was different. The experience of Cindy Breakspeare (Miss Jamaica) and Jennifer Hosten (Grenada) in winning Miss World had raised the expectations of contestants - they were determined to pursue a career in the beauty industry. The stakes were raised, commercial sponsorship introduced, and a ready-made industry was reborn.

Sammy Jay Holder dominated the industry for a few years from 1975 and was able to reproduce the format of the early JOFFA shows. Because there was insignificant competition, the Miss West Indian title drew the best entry, including nationally known models. The standard of modelling could not be matched either, and shortly after, African-Caribbean beauty contests declined further, though their increased popularity seemed to suggest otherwise in the short-term.

Beverley Heath, Yana Francois and Veronica White, won Miss West Indian in consecutive years. Since then, however, professional models have rarely sought such titles, and are not really welcomed. From the start of the 1980s, fashion and beauty contests parted company. Few, if any achieved any degree of success in the media. The spectacle of promotion overshadowed individual participants and the more the industry expanded, the more the vein of quality diminished.

A tide of luck came to the industry with profits from Nigerian oil and American beauty products. These were invested chiefly to enhance shows as entertainment. More and more contestants were attracted by the apparent glamour, but few had the professional standards of their predecessors. Several titles flourished where there had been only one, as competitors fought for limited pickings. What appeared, was a renewed approach in the modelling field, with so-called 'modelling schools' and agencies mushrooming in the community, with few applicants refused. A sub-culture now developed in which contests were used to attract people to the schools and agencies that competed for increased title-holders than their rivals.

These units of enterprise existed to provide entrants for various competitions. Serious-minded models gave the whole confusing business a wider berth.

Community fashion shows provide an invaluable outlet for designers and aspiring models who have the opportunity to test the quality of their productions. Even so, these events should not be mistaken for the real thing, particularly when those concerned do not have the necessary physical criteria. There is a new generation of students and trainees who are determined to be professionals in the fashion and beauty industry - today described as the 'cultural industries' by the European funding regime. Their quest for excellence lies in their exceptional flair and creativity.

By the early 1990s, the black community began to make further inroads into the fashion industry. Naiomi Campbell's rise to international stardom catapulted others to follow. Model Christine Denham has conquered the international catwalks, appeared in pop videos with superstars and is now a scriptwriter. In 1991 she heralded the Shaven Look: *In those days, they would only look at a Black girl if she had European weaves and small features and I really wanted to change all that. I feel that we are such a beautiful race, so why should we conform to European looks?*

In 1994, several models organised by the African Design Centre celebrated Afro-ethnicity with an impressive array of outfits worn by a bevy of African-Caribbean young women. One outstanding participant was Celina Sylvia Hewitt who was born to Caribbean parents, but who grew up in east London. Now pursing a career in nursery nursing, Celina is a product of Laurie Small Modelling School's fashion. She is however not the traditional young model. She insists that women do not have to wear swimsuits to accentuate their beauty. "Women can demonstrate sharper grace, charm and poise with a range of colourfully-styled apparel".

The fusion of cultures has generated a unique blend of African, Asian and European styles. Jamaica was praised as being the rising centre of international fashion on one of the Annual Clothes Show programmes on BBC television some years ago. Several designers featured had learnt their craft in the United Kingdom but had returned to the Caribbean when they found that opportunities in Britain were not what they had anticipated. Cindy Breakspeare, the former Miss World, has done much to publicise the interest in the Caribbean.

Britain's contribution, as the cross-roads between our home countries, the US and Western Europe, has been most pronounced in hair and beauty products. That will constitute a separate chapter. Perhaps this success has been brought about by a hard-core group of specialists taking the lead in the industry, instead of leaving it to outside entrepreneurs.

The fashion industry has also taken on a new dimension. Departmental stores with household names use the services of models to promote their merchandise. While this may lack the glamorous appeal to those who seek public recognition, it offers those on the catwalk in some instances greater financial rewards. Marks & Spencer employed Pauline Bryan and Kathy Alexis almost twenty years ago and Beverley Keen, an early Miss Dyke & Dryden beauty queen, was engaged similarly by C& A.

The Beauty Queen with Tessa Sanderson

The Author in conversation with
Brenda Emanus and Jodie Hanson-Norte

Labour and Capital

When facilities for education, health, housing, business organisations and professional recognition were denied, Commonwealth immigrants sought representation from the trade union system. The labour movement thus became an organ of structural and social change for the thousands who migrated to Britain. Like him or loathe him, the manual worker had to get on with his shop steward or the equivalent. It was this official who made recommendations for more favourable conditions of work and service through the local union branch. At least in theory the new arrivals started on the same footing as his neighbour.

Some immigrants of the 1950s and 1960s had prior experience of trade union power in their homeland. The battles for recognition were not the same as they were for white workers. The formation of effective trade unions in the Caribbean were linked to the struggle for political independence and self-government. Respect for a successful labour organiser draws on the electorate's loyalty to a candidate considered suitable for political power. A typical example was Sir Eric Gairy, who won the appreciation of the Grenadian people for his trade union activities before turning to politics.

The organisation of Jamaican sugar cane workers in the late 1930s was seen as a landmark in the island's move towards self-rule and in Sir Alexander Bustamante's career. This flamboyant personality captured the imagination of the agricultural workers, as did his colleague and long-time rival, Norman Manley, in more traditional politics. English people are often confused that an essentially capitalist party can be called the (Jamaica) Labour Party and be supported by a substantial sector of the working class. This is because its history is rooted in the agricultural rather than the industrial sector.

One should not give the distinct impression however, that all British trade unions welcomed us with open arms. In fact some of the earliest struggles were against local branches who considered that their primary duty was to protect existing members against the influx of outside workers. They feared that the immigrants would be persuaded to work for lower wages, and that the increase in the potential labour force would be a prelude to widespread unemployment. Those industries vulnerable to recession were particularly apprehensive. They considered the situation as a challenge.

Enoch Powell's 'rivers of blood' speech in 1968 was delivered in the West Midlands where, four years earlier, Peter Griffiths had won the Smethwick seat for the Conservatives, against the national trend in the general election, through his association with the slogan 'if you want a nigger for a neighbour, vote Liberal or Labour'. He was certain of the sympathy of the workers in the motor industry who were facing cutbacks in the labour force. London dockers who saw their position of European paramountcy lost to Rotterdam and Amsterdam, marched in support of Powell. Nevertheless, shop stewards needed our votes to retain their positions. Besides, they understood more than anyone else that the African-Caribbean workers received their first experience of leadership at local level within their workplace. Indeed, in some sectors they formed the majority members of staff. During the post-war expansion, British transport and health authorities conducted a special recruitment drive for bus drivers, conductors and nurses from Jamaica and Barbados, many of whom lived near to their workplace. This situation encouraged the potential development of ghettos. Industries too, such as car manufacturing, relocated to more developed urban areas, taking the bulk of their workers with them.

Promotion was slow for professionals in the trade union movement because it involved experience and knowledge of most, if not all of its branches. A leader therefore, becomes a recognisable public figure only after many years of service. Because African-Caribbean people made their entry into British labour unions at a comparatively late stage, very few have attracted national attention. This however is changing and will continue to do so in the years to come. It is interesting to note that the campaign for more open government, for equal opportunity and for more diversity in all fields of human endeavour are beginning attract some young, bright, politically aware people into following a trade union career.

Louis Mahoney who was a former vice president of Equity, the actor's union, was the first black spokesman of the present generation to make an impression as a speaker at the annual conference of the Trades Union Congress. Ironically, it was an actor who pleaded for greater representation for black people in industry. During the 1950s, Mahoney taught maths, English and biology in West Ham. Like acting, it was also the communications profession which brought black officers to public attention.

Guyanese Trevor Phillips, who is now Chair of the Commission for Racial Equality, is a former president of the National Union of Students (an organisation in which his older brother, Mike was involved). Trevor was known best as presenter and editor of current affairs. He featured on programmes such as *Skin, Black on Black, Club Mix, The Making of Britain* and *This Week*. His recent weekly television slot, The London Programme was exceedingly informative and had an intellectual following. His ability to focus ethnic and racial issues within the framework of mainstream society is indeed a fitting tribute to Phillip's prior experience in student union activism. His political position of influence as Chairman of the GLA, and now Chairman of the CRE adds another significant rung to his career.

South African Lionel Morrison served as president of the National Union of Journalists in 1987/1988, a similar body of the multi-racial South African Union of Journalists, before his escape from that country in 1960. He travelled in Africa, Asia, Latin America and Europe, before settling in Britain in 1969. Morrison has worked in a number of media-related positions. He was Principal Information Officer for the CRE after showing it was possible (though rare) for a journalist to transfer from the ethnic to the national press. Apart from organising specialist courses in journalism, at the time of writing, he was chairman of the Notting Hill Housing Association.

Bill Morris is today the most distinguished contemporary trade unionist. He is the general secretary of probably the most powerful and influential union in the country - the Transport and General Workers Union (TGWU). Ron Todd, Bill's immediate predecessor, was considered to be King maker and the "power behind the throne".

Morris left Jamaica over forty years ago and came into the trade union movement through his regional work in Nottingham. The unassuming Morris is level headed and blessed with a perceptive mind. He does not suffer fools gladly. His debating skills are graced with a calm that destroys opponents without hurt.

In 1985, he joined the T&G and by 1983, he had become a shop steward at Hardy Spicer, an engineering company where he worked and was destined for the top. He was elected to serve as a member of the General Executive Council, the Union's governing body, before being appointed as a full time official in 1973.

In 1979, he was appointed National Secretary of the Passenger Services Trade Group, representing bus workers throughout the United Kingdom. His appointment as Deputy General Secretary in 1986 was followed by a change in the law under which he was re-elected to that position in 1990. Through a membership ballot he was elected to the Union's most senior post, that of General Secretary, in 1991. In 1979, he fought a successful campaign for re-election.

As Deputy General Secretary, he was given responsibility for education and the equalities brief.

During this time he became a commissioner on the Commission for Racial Equality, a position that he held for seven years. He also served as a member of both the Independent Broadcasting Authority's General Advisory Council and the British Broadcasting Corporation's Advisory Board.

As a senior officer, he has been a member of the General Council of Trades Union Congress for fourteen years, serving on its executive committee and chairing tasks groups set up to deal with representation at work and promoting trade unionism.

A past member of the Advisory Arbitration and Conciliation Service, he currently sits on the Executive Board of the International Transport Workers Federation, and is a non-Executive Director of the Bank of England. He also serves on the Employment Appeals Tribunal and is a member of the Commission for Integrated Transport. His most recent appointment was to membership of the Architect's Registration Board. Having described education as his passion, he was extremely proud to have been appointed as Chancellor of U-Tech, the University of Technology in Jamaica. He has been awarded honorary degrees from several UK universities.

In 1995, the opposition Labour Party tried to realign the relationship between itself and the TUC. Jack Romney and his supporters fought gallantly to oust Morris but failed miserably. The election bid was described in sections of the media as the Battle of the Anglo-Caribbean Bulge. The public knew little of how Morris's leadership helped to unify and sustain the TGWU against the backdrop of reduced union powers brought about by tough anti-labour legislation more than a decade ago. It was not surprising that the inevitable took place - the dynamic and ebullient Morris was unanimously elected as General Secretary of the TGWU.

The first organisers of labour in Britain were made less welcome. William Cuffay participated in the founding of the Metropolitan Tailors Charter Association in 1839, during the time of the Chartist agitation. He became the country's leading Chartist spokesman and was appointed to the interim executive of the Metropolitan Delegate Council when the national leaders were under arrest. Cuffay was a London delegate to the National Convention of the Chartists in 1848, which was known as the year of revolutions, because of the violent unrest, which swept across Europe and overthrew kings and governments.

William was elected to chair the committee to manage the procession taking a petition to the House of Commons but the march was abandoned. Thereafter, he turned towards more insurrectionary tactics and was arrested. He was sentenced and then deported to Tasmania, where he spent the rest of his life. He was permitted to continue his tailoring profession, although his reputation as a protest organiser was publicly acclaimed. Australia was then an ethnic melting pot in which four decades later, Sam Morris became the first West Indian to play in a Test match and Peter Jackson emerged as the greatest heavyweight boxer of his age.

Even before the era of mass immigration, the TUC in 1930 passed a resolution that "this Congress views with alarm the continued employment of alien and undesirable coloured labour on British ships to the detriment of British seamen and calls upon the government to use all of their powers to provide remedial action". Surprisingly, racial disturbances during the inter-war period centred on the ports, which, once associated with the Slave Trade, had the longest established black population, many of whom had returned to the sea for their jobs.

While Bill Morris enjoyed national recognition, others made significant inroads regionally. Councillor Ronald Browne became treasurer of the Chiswick branch of the Electrical Engineers Technicians and Plumbing Union. Councillor Henry Cleghorn held various district offices with the National Union of Railwaymen. Councillor Franklyn Georges was a member of the national committee of the National Union of Public Employees (NUPE). Barbadian Eddic Niles was the first black branch secretary of the union, while Bernie Grant was an area officer of the organisation before being elected a Labour MP in the mid-1980s.

Francis Walker, was the first West Indian to be elected branch secretary and chairman of the Associated Society of Locomotive Engineers and Firemen, and was a delegate member on the union's negotiating team. He was the first West Indian to attend the Chairmen and Secretaries Conference. While he held office between 1970 and 1972, Walker was recognised for encouraging other black people to participate actively in trade unionism. This of course helped to influence the careers of many black employees at the time.

It would be appropriate to record here Lord Pitt's presidency of the British Medical Association, even though his political activities are mentioned in other sections of this book. The success of African-Caribbean unionists at the national level was due to their enduring sacrifice and struggle to represent fellow employees against systematic injustice in the workplace. Quoting from an article in 'Third World Impact':-

"The institutions of the British labour movement cannot escape the scrutiny of anti-racists. Indeed it would be astonishing, given the history of Britain and its colonies, if organisations based on the British working class were not to some extent polluted by racial discrimination.... Hence the great dilemma of black people in the labour movement. On the one hand it exists to promote social change, to eradicate class divisions and to empower the powerless. On the other hand, it is itself distorted by the racism of the social order it is challenging. It would seem that black people should be looking to direct and lead the movement, and notwithstanding they should be protesting at its own discrimination and injustices."

The TGWU boss considered that the problem was not the ideas of change, but the will to implement change.

I have explained already how difficult it has been for African-Caribbean people to raise capital for business start-ups, to buy property or even finance the costly journeys back to the West Indies for emergencies such as illness or death. Financing through the "partner system" was the most common method of raising cash for specific purposes.

This type of commercial venture is considered by some to be hazardous for a mobile immigrant community. A partner may move on after drawing his/her lump sum and before paying his/her full number of instalments, or the banker could move. The fact that the system survived such anxieties is ample testimony to the general honesty of those involved. This practice also demonstrates that the Enterprise Culture was rooted in African-Caribbean communities long before the very term gained modern currency.

The next step in the sophistication of social credit, was a similar self-serving device introduced by Frank Villiers, the Managing Director of the Credit Union League of Great Britain at the time. He was a qualified accountant and Chartered Secretary and came to Britain from Jamaica at the turn of the 1960s. He worked as a consultant with a City firm and was involved in credit unions since 1943. He told the first edition of West Indians in Great Britain that he wanted us, as pioneers, to enjoy the fruits of our labours, that the movement was founded by West Indians in Britain, and that social credit could be the answer to the lack of expansion in commerce. Several businessmen engaged Frank as an advisor on accounts and finance.

Denzie McKevin Hazell, a graduate from the University of London, was President of the International Credit Union. He was also secretary of the St. Vincent Association. He founded the Pelican Finance Co., and Pelican Estate Agency as part of his ambition to create a financial economic institution for the benefit of the community. He expressed the wish that black people would give more moral and financial support to their businesses. The African-Caribbean population demanded more specialist financial services since they were keen on improving their general well being in Britain.

Brown and White Incorporated were practising in North London by the early 1970s. Gerry Brown, a Jamaican, studied banking at the North London Polytechnic, and was a member of the West Indian National Association, one of the first organisations which brought West Indians together irrespective of territorial background. The younger generation today, born here and classified across the board as 'black', may be surprised at the difficulty experienced in breaking down territorial differences. This attitude which is often described as 'insularity' dogged even the West Indies cricket team during the 1970s and early 1980.

There was also a growing body of Caribbean insurance advisors. Cecil Chanderbham, an active member of the Lions Club, arrived in Britain as a manager of the Caribbean Atlantic Life Assurance. Clement Culley from Guyana, however, worked himself from ledger clerk to inspector. He was later appointed agency manager of the Colonial Life Assurance Co. Ltd. Fitzroy Jones, originally from St. Kitts, was an insurance broker with Easton Agencies. Malcolm Saunders from the island worked for Crown Life Assurance and Caribbean Atlantic before launching his company - Malrose Services Limited.

Joe Whitter was the best-known property developer of the early years. He operated at a time when West Indians were having difficulty in obtaining a conventional mortgage for properties, either in Britain or in the Caribbean. A Jamaican, he was based in South-East London, and was a member of the West Indian League and WISC. For some years, Whitter was a celebrated personality in the area in which he worked. He returned to Jamaica in the 1970s and manages his huge estate, "*Ironshore*", at Montego Bay.

A gallant attempt in trying to get a Caribbean financial institution off the ground in the UK, known as the First Partnership Bank, has been a major disappointment for the community.

The First Partnership Bank project was launched by Sir George Young. The aim of the project was to help resolve problems faced by Black and ethnic minority entrepreneurs in establishing businesses through a viable financial institutional framework. The concept was developed through a steering committee in the London boroughs of Hackney, Haringey and Lambeth and the cities of Bristol and Birmingham. Barbadian-born Sam Springer, MBE., DI, chaired the Committee. Educated in the Caribbean where he owned and managed a small tourist business, he came to England in 1955. He served on a number of statutory and voluntary bodies since 1967. In particular he was a member of the Economic Development Staff of the Hackney London Borough Council, its Equal Opportunities Committees, the North Metropolitan Conciliation Committee of the Race Relations Board, the Home Secretary's Advisory Council on Race Relations and the Industrial and Employment Appeal Tribunals. Springer's influence was enormous. In 1978 he was appointed additional Commissioner to investigate employment policies of the National Bus Company.

Springer received public acclaim when he was elected the first black Mayor of Hackney in 1982. In that capacity he came to appreciate the need to develop a black financial institution and later led a delegation to the US to research the potential for such a venture. Four years on, he was leader of another delegation to Dallas, Texas, to examine trading possibilities between the ethnic minorities in the US and the United Kingdom. His other awards include the Freedom of the City of London and appointment as Deputy Lord Lieutenant of Greater London.

Hercules Emmanuel Cotter MBE, MBA, who was born in St. Lucia and studied economic development in the US, was also a pioneer of the First Partnership Bank. He was the Economic Development Manager for Hackney's Economic Development Unit, which provided guidance, and support for the establishment of small businesses in the Borough. Manny, as he is affectionately known, was instrumental in persuading the City of London Polytechnic to introduce a management training unit to cater for black entrepreneurs. His extraordinary business skills are well known and widely respected across the country.

Before joining Hackney Council, he ran a successful clothing company in the Borough developing a number of specialist skills and employment in the area.

His success in Hackney led to being head hunted as Executive Director for the North London Business Development Agency (NLBDA), a government sponsored body resulting from Lord Scarman's report arising out of the Brixton riots. His tenure at the Agency was a resounding success, helping to found over some three thousand small businesses across a broad area of activity earning even greater respect from the whole community. Currently he serves his country in the capacity of High Commissioner for the UK and Europe.

In the area of capital appreciation, success of the first arrivals could be measured by their acquisition of property. Initially, they shared rooms, then moved into one of their own and later purchased apartments or flats. As funds became available, many West Indians bought larger properties to accommodate relatives - children, parents/grandparents, younger brothers and sisters - from the Caribbean.

In the area of acquired wealth, the ownership of property is by far the single most valuable asset held by the black community, which today is valued in billions of pounds. The economics of buying was well founded. In the first place the amounts paid out in rents went towards paying the mortgage for the house. Secondly some rooms were rented, generating additional income which became a source for funding other enterprises.

As a percentage of the population, black home ownership is indicative of the will and ability to improve the quality of life by their own efforts, given the opportunity to do so. This marvellous enterprising effort has not been without countless discriminatory practises. Higher prices and loaded insurance policies, in some cases, to cover their homes.

Considering where we have come from, buying and selling property at a profit provided the major source of funding for other enterprises and was a way around some uncaring, and unhelpful banks.

The home was where organising business matters and employment could be practised when opportunity was denied elsewhere. At first, West Indians had little or no choice whatsoever in the working environment. A carpenter for example, pressed into service as a bus conductor, found expression in making beautiful items of furniture for his home. The best carpenter I know had cleaned industrial chimneys, but yet his house was full of exquisite woodwork creations.

Building a sound and strong black economic base in Britain is only a matter of time. It is clear from reading this book to see that the groundwork is steadily being laid. We have seen from the early days in Brixton, the rise of sole traders and family run businesses. That same pattern of progress is taking place across the length and breath of the country.

I have been privileged to have had my own company's experience that led in many directions to working with the community in a number of organisations, as Chairman of the (UK) Caribbean Chamber of Commerce, Chairman of The North London Business Development Agency, Chair of Stonebridge Housing Action Trust, and the North London Training and Enterprise Board, and can accurately gage the passion with which the spirit of enterprise has pervaded the new generation who are better equipped, better educated and therefore better able to take black business to the next level.

The reader will readily note the very refreshing mix of enterprises into which people are now engaged, all of which offers opportunities for growth. Examples of this happening are already taking place by way of buying into franchises, supplying chain stores, and entry into the capital markets.

Finally, we have seen that hard won capital appreciation exists in property, and how this huge wealth will be used is left to be seen. One thing for sure is that a culture of enterprise is in place, and it is this pragmatic approach and hard work, more than anything else, which will drive the community in attaining its place in the business and commercial life of the nation.

Religion

Two issues which sometimes create sharp divisions between individuals and societies are politics and religion, with the latter being more controversial because of its ranging beliefs, denominational faiths, histories and cultures. The strength of one's faith is a very important factor. This chapter will therefore, make references to notable persons in the African Caribbean community who, through their religion and beliefs, have influenced change in business practices and society in general in Britain.

Black British churches lead the way towards religious revival and, to a very large extent, have influenced both the style of worship and the type of congregation compared with established churches. To a large extent, people in Britain and in the Caribbean were brought up along the same traditional Christian principles, sharing the same act of fellowship, similar creeds, rituals, and the Holy Scriptures. On the face of it, nothing was amiss, acts of brotherhood and sisterhood belonged to one big Christian family wherever they may be.

Early Christian immigrants expected to find acceptance by established congregations in the manner and fashion they practised at home, but they felt disappointed by the way white Christians treated them. I am sure in most cases that what seemed, as a rebuff was not intentional but possibly a culture clash between the immigrant and the indigenous population.

Worship in a typical white environment is more often than not calm and reserved lasting one hour on average, against a typical Caribbean form of worship lasting some three hours, punctuated at times by verbal rejoicing if the worshipper feels led by the spirit to do so.

This contrast in expressing one's faith comes down to customs, habits and behavioural norms across the whole Christian community, whether in the UK or the Caribbean. I must add however that it is the newer revivalist churches that differ more profoundly in their ways of worship than the long established churches.

In considering the alienation expressed by some immigrants, Caribbean communities are relatively small where members knew each other, compared to the huge conurbations in which village people were suddenly exposed to. There are some exceptions for cities like Port-of-Spain, Kingston, and Georgetown, towns with distinctive characteristics, though nothing quite like the urban sprawl of London straddling both sides of the

Thames. Our Caribbean Christian experiences are those passed down during colonial times. For example, the tradition of marriage, baptism, communion and confirmation, all reflect religious tradition with the UK.

The initial rejection and isolation faced by Caribbean immigrants from the host community, forced the former into worship with congregations of traditional ethnic and racial composition. It meant for example that Caribbean people of differing faiths worshipped together, Methodists, Baptists, Moravians or Pentecostals, as a means of common fellowship.

The Roman Catholic Church is visible throughout the Caribbean, particularly where there are French and Spanish influences. English-speaking territories such as Barbados, Guyana and Montserrat, have a strong Anglican community alongside other non-conformist faiths, such as the Baptists, Congregationalists and Methodists. There are, however, a multitude of revivalist churches throughout the region.

In dealing with religion it must not be overlooked that Guyana and Trinidad, for example, have impressive temples and mosques to cater for the spiritual needs of their Hindu and Muslim communities, while synagogues are equally common for Jews.

Religion is a source of comfort for those affected most by injustices, and those who have no significant representation in the political establishment. It was no accident, therefore, that the greatest opposition against apartheid in South Africa, came from church leaders such as Archbishop Desmond Tutu and Dr Allan Boesak.

The foundations of segregation in the southern part of the US were undermined by the stirring advocacy of civil rights leaders. Dr. Martin Luther King and Ralph Abernathy were both influential and dedicated Baptist Ministers. Presidential aspirant, Jesse Jackson, started his public life as a religious orator. There are many in Britain who consider that a clergyman of similar convictions, rather than the Local Government and our Parliamentary machinery, would best serve the interest of the African Caribbean community.

From the early 1970s, the black led Churches have inspired a renaissance and positive growth in worship among the immigrant community in Britain.

Inevitably, a youthful community exposed to all kinds of influences identified with conventional behaviour, the mode of dress, speech and general custom of Rastafarianism. (It must be remembered that it became difficult to determine the true Rasta from the hangers on.) This gave the young a sense of identity and a personality glamorised by the popularity of reggae superstar, Bob Marley. Rastafarianism represented protest and resistance to deprivation in the inner cities of England.

Apart from its religious impact, Rastafarianism played a cultural role in moulding members of the African Diaspora through a shared sense of cultural heritage. Although their traditions were frequently mocked, devotees made it known to their white neighbours, the importance of Caribbean cultural heritage and the recognition it should be accorded in Britain. The Rastas cannot be ignored - they have a permanent place in our history. To date, a handful of Europeans have joined the faith and emulated some of its popular traditions, the wearing of extended locks, partaking in ethnic foods and chanting 'I-Man' vibrations (music).

Pentecostal followers and adherents are the fastest growing of the Caribbean churches. Pastoral leadership comes from the black middle classes, the professions and small business owners. It draws its membership from a cross section of the community, and fills a great consoling need. Culturally, they are the backbone of traditional Caribbean society. They fulfil the community's thirst for joyful worship, which imparts a sense of belonging and spiritual togetherness greatly prized by its members.

Even the most sympathetic of Anglo-Saxons is inclined to label all Third World peoples as radical and socialist in outlook. Ten to fifteen years ago this stereotype seemed true. Yet the Christian emphasis on personal responsibility for decency and morality is quite the opposite and leads directly to the popularity of the churches. In fact most Caribbean leaders were well versed in the Bible, and such knowledge is proven during their political hustings. This tends to have a positive effect on the electorate.

One should not get the distinct impression that African Caribbean people have turned away from established Christian denominations. When Barbadian-born Bishop Wilfred Woods, rose to an influential position in the Church of England, Roman Catholics from Trinidad, St. Lucia, Dominica and Jamaica, supported him in faith in large numbers. Nevertheless, the dynamism and spiritual confidence has been provided mainly by those churches which are new to Britain and new in their exposition of the gospel.

It is appropriate to explain here my own position on the importance of faith as an ingredient of business practice and for life as a whole. My views are summed up in a speech I made at Trinity at Bowes in London on 23rd May 1982, from which the following extract is taken:-

"Some of the questions that commonly face a Christian in business life are -

Does your faith really matter? What relationship is there between faith and making money? Is it not that a business exists to benefit its shareholders and its employees? As a Christian my perception is different - John chapter 6 verse 28 asks: What shall we do that we may work the work of God? As a Christian, while recognising the contribution of both employer and employee, I place emphasis on the element of service to others, understanding that all our work must be for the glory of God. This, I believe, is the answer to the question."

I find that faith in business makes a tremendous difference: prayer before making important decisions gives me an inner confidence about the decision to be made. Faith in business enriches the quality of life. It acknowledges the skills with which you are endowed, materials for our use and the opportunity to meet the needs of others. Proverbs chapter 16 verse 3 puts it: 'commit your works to the Lord'. Faith in business is a living testimony by example in dealing with colleagues and the team around you, by always seeking ways of improved efficiency, both in terms of quality and keen prices, and the responsibility of ensuring that each member of your team is involved, contributing well and paid well.

In short, it is the Christian who sets the standards that should be followed in industry and commerce - there are, of course, shortcomings at times - the ideal may not be attainable but it is just in situations like these that you rejoice in the fact that you have your faith.

My experience of religion goes back a very long way - to my childhood in Montserrat. It is said that a person's character is formed in those early years. Not surprisingly therefore, faith and religion remains an important part of my life, it could not be otherwise.

I am happy to explain that I am, in fact, a product of Methodist missionary work in the Caribbean. You may well ask - How? Well, during my formative years all the schools were church schools and without the churches there would have been no schools as they were then. I might tell you too, that my mother was a Methodist and my father, Church of England - and I chose to follow in her footsteps.

Apart from my mother, two of my uncles, who were also local preachers, had a significant influence on me and it was while attending one of the great missionary revival evenings and during the singing of 'Bringing in the Sheaves' that my heart was strangely touched.

Reflecting on Methodism on the island, the church and the community were one. It was vibrant and joyous inter-action of caring, sharing and mutual respect. The church seasons - Christmas, Easter and Harvest-time - were times of great rejoicing, for wearing your Sunday best and giving God the best. In celebrating harvests, the churches looked somewhat like a forest of fruits, vegetables, flowers and cotton. Some of the produce went to the poor and the needy, while the remainder were sold to maintain the minister and the church.

If you conjure up in your mind a picture of the *Sound of Music*, you would capture the echoing of the great favourite hymns like 'We plough the fields and scatter' and 'Come ye thankful people come' across the hills and valleys. These were wonderful memories which I cannot help recalling. I might add that I have, over the years, remained loyal to my religion and settled into the pattern of worship at The Bourne, unlike some of my colleagues.

Churches in the Caribbean are characterised by praise, joy and sometimes emotional participation. Singing plays an important part of their worship, and has provided a nursery for several popular singers and musicians. This vibrant attitude to religion, which English audiences glimpsed in the show *Black Nativity* which toured here in the 1960s, is further evidence that although our brand of Christianity was handed down from Europe, the African influence has been assimilated - and is ever present.

There is debate on whether gospel music should be a broader church. This type of music thrived on the closed church circuit since black churches were established in the UK. Young Christians in the black community are learning from their counterparts across the Atlantic. The term British Gospel Music was coined in the mid-80s to describe the differences between the US and UK influences on Black gospel. British black gospel has a base of the American equivalent - with a dash of calypso and reggae, and sprinkles of rock-and-roll.

During 1984 the broadcasting and popularity of black gospel music escalated beyond precedent, except perhaps for that solitary peak in the summer of 1969 when the Edwin Hawkins Singers topped the UK charts with 'Oh Happy Day'. The main reasons for this new popularity may be found in social changes, arising out of a more outward looking society. This may be one contributory factor, at least in London. The first regular gospel music programme on British radio - broadcast initially on Sunday nights from February 1984 by radio station JFM- was significant.

More gospel airplay followed when BBC Radio One launched Gary

Byrd's *Sweet Inspiration* show, and later Capital Radio scheduled *When The Spirit Moves,* hosted by Al Matthews. Black gospel singers, British and American, gained television appearances.

In November 1995, the National Gospel Music Awards were held in the UK and the UK Female Artist of the Year went to Dawn Thomas, while the UK Choir of the Year went to the London Adventist Chorale. They were the first Black gospel choir to win the Sainsbury's Choir of the Year competition in 1995.

The explanation of religion in the Caribbean is essential in understanding the present position in the United Kingdom. The cohesive integration, which we knew back home, was shared by social and religious values. As has been explained earlier, the congregation, the family, neighbours and colleagues at school and at work were very much the same people who also came from the same background.   In the case of youngsters who were born and bred in Britain, they are subjected to different and conflicting influences - in effect, their socialisation process is quite dissimilar.

Schools have taken over much of the responsibility for teaching moral and religious instructions, which is frequently at variance with Caribbean parents.

The values reflected by television programmes and the newspapers provide yet another alternative interpretation. Small wonder that children are confused, and this has led, in some cases, to frustration and lack of understanding in families and communities, which are expected to be united.

It is neither my wish nor intention to comment on the respective merits of various religious creeds. They provide education and conform to traditional family ties and community kinship. They also offer incentive to combat lawlessness. Evil cannot take possession of a highly spirited person or a God-fearing individual. Those misguided souls are likely to be at the mercy of evil forces.

The impressive record of the John Loughborough School (JLS) in Tottenham, north London, is often cited as a wonderful example of religious education and moral upliftment. It may seem a paradox, but comprehensive schools in general, have been preferred to private because the latter have been the bastions of traditional privilege and advantage. Even so, religious and ethnic groups regard specialised private schooling as providing a rare chance to prevent their own culture from being submerged to the point of oblivion.

The JLS was opened in April 1980 and is operated solely on tuition fees and substantial subsidies from the Seventh-day Adventist Church. Boys and girls from 9 to 18 years old are accepted from all faiths. The citation of an award to the former headmaster, Keith Davidson, refers to him giving the incentive to each child and encouraging them to go 'the extra mile. He fosters excellence among his young charges for them to meet minimum requirements - as prescribed by other such institutions.

Mr. Davidson came to England as a teenager and acquired experience in posts as an accounts clerk, a teacher and bursar at the school. He was promoted headmaster in 1985, holding degrees in business studies and education administration. The older generation schooled in the Caribbean feel that British society has taken away much of the authority of parents and teachers, and may have seen an echo of their own sentiments in the headmaster's statement of his personal beliefs.

His overall aim was to engender self-confidence and self-worth in children, teaching them to develop positive aspects of their personality. To achieve this, he strove for high quality teaching with a staff who acted as role models - that is, successful black adults in society. It is evident that alienation of the individual, and the consequent loss of identity observed by specialists in many professions are at the root of most social problems.

In recent years, evangelism has become a wave of spiritual enlightenment. Jamaican-born Rev. Joel Edwards is the first black person to be appointed general director of the Evangelical Alliance UK. The EA represents the interest of 56,000 members and 3,500 churches.

A New Testament Church of God minister, he studied theology at the London Bible College in the early 1970s. At the college, he said, the people could not believe I had never heard of the great British theologians whom they revered. They never expected we had such a depth and breadth of religion.

Edwards previously worked as a probation officer for nearly ten years, mainly in north London. In 1996, the EA celebrated its 50th anniversary.

Chair of the Moss Side Women's Action Forum is Louise Da Codia, who was a former nurse and a Christian devotee. She acknowledges the late Dr. Martin Luther King as a role model. I was taught that you were a child of God from an early age. She believes that in the Caribbean, you are instilled with a sense of worth that has been denied to the black population in Britain. She sits on the Synod - the policy-making body of the Church of England.

One of the Black church's most successful economic achievements has been the founding of the Pentecostal Credit Union (PCU). Twenty-three years ago the Reverend Carmel Jones, a Church of God in Christ minister, successfully helped to empower his flock economically - something the PCU succeeded in doing. At the time of writing, the PCU had a membership of 1,800 with assets totalling £2.25 million.

Missionary work in reverse is now taking place in the UK. A newly qualified Methodist minister explained, on graduation, to his friends that he was thinking of going into missionary work in Africa, and was admonished by his people, telling him that this is where he was needed and that he should stay, and he did.

The established churches leadership in the UK have taken a sympathetic view on race and community relations, which can be seen by their pronouncements on apartheid in South African and other flashpoints around the world. The same all embracing impact is yet to make its mark decisively on stable race relations here in the UK.

Throughout this chapter, I have referred to the historical context of Christianity in the Caribbean, and its central place in the life of the majority in our communities.

It is not entirely coincidental that the development in African Caribbean enterprise is occurring alongside renewal and religious growth. Faith has given us the confidence to overcome situations that at times seem impossible to the faithless.

The Rev. Ola Vincent Odulele of the Glory Bible Church, stresses that Churches can facilitate economic development within the black community, not only by funding local business ventures, but also by encouraging congregations to support other black businesses.

We are yet to see a religious leader of the stature of a Dr Martin Luther King or Bishop Desmond Tutu, but this may not be long in coming, for the spirit enterprise that ministers to the body as well as the soul is alive and well in the black community.

The Services

Caribbean peoples of all races have played a prominent role in the defence and maintenance of the British realm. The army and the navy provided an outlet from poverty under colonial rule. The difference between the merchant and the (military) navy was not as it is today. Nor was the service in war limited to men. In recent times, the late Mary Seacole's contribution to nursing at the height of the Crimean War has been recognised in sections of the local press. The media spotlight on Florence Nightingale, however, overshadowed her distinctive efforts.

Seacole came to London in 1853 from Jamaica, where she opened a hotel, which soon became a makeshift shop, pharmacy and hospital. She had much success in curing cholera with her herbal medicines. The British could only look in awe. She is still revered today by many older Caribbean nationals, especially nurses and community leaders. Liverpool is to pay homage by erecting a statute of Seacole.

The military successes of Toussaint L'Ouverture, Jean-Jacques Dessalines and Henri Christophe in Haiti's slave revolt and the ensuing war of independence, as well as the guerrilla tactics of the Jamaican Maroons, proved that African-Caribbean people had martial ability.

It was not so long ago, that a former South African fast bowler raised a furore in the cricket press after alleging that there were no war graves for fallen Caribbean soldiers in the last two world wars. The profound nature of the response showed how widespread was our contribution to the war effort. It was our service in these conflicts which provided the impetus for our presence in Britain in the first place, temporarily before later consideration was given to settling. We earned the right of settlers by virtue of being citizens of the Empire, and more specifically by shedding blood.

The declared intention of the racist Nazi regime was enough for Caribbean people from across the whole social structure to volunteer for the Second World War. The distinguished Barbadian cricketer, Everton Weekes (one of the three Ws - the others being Sir Frank Worrell and Sir Clyde Walcott), for example, was part of the Caribbean Regiment. It is noteworthy that part of the leadership, which provided the framework of a Caribbean community in the United Kingdom in the 1950s, developed honed administrative skills in wartime service. Others represented untold and unsung heroes.

The West Indian Ex-Servicemen's Association (WIESA) is a respected and vibrant organisation that has honoured the memory of those who fought during the war. Their campaigns attest to the importance of this organisation. Veteran soldiers participate in the annual Remembrance Day celebrations at the Cenotaph. Mrs. Connie Mark, who is a dynamic community leader, is probably among the few, if not the only Caribbean woman, to march in the November parade. It should not be forgotten that many of us chose to bury our differences and fight alongside Britain for a common cause at a time when the Caribbean was struggling for Political Independence and self-government.

Mrs Connie Mark was attached to the Royal Army Medical Corps and after working there for ten years was awarded the War Medal. She is vigorously involved in promoting Caribbean history, cooking and culture. She is a member of the British Caribbean Association, the Anti-Racist Committee, Founder friends of Mary Seacole and WIESA. Some years ago, she mounted a photo exhibition depicting her range of community activities. Her experiences as a black woman in a white army are fascinating to listen to. She was born in Jamaica and worked as a medical secretary by profession.

Writing in the UK edition of the Jamaican Gleaner's Special War Memories features to mark the fiftieth anniversary of the outbreak of the Second World War, Sam King recalled that Jamaica pledged support within 24 hours of Britain's declaration of war, and observed that it was common for Trinidadian seamen to be torpedoed because of the vital oil they were transporting. He observed that West Indians died in every theatre of war, from Iceland to the Pacific, and remarked that men like Samuda, Wint, Bryan (killed in action) and others were always encouraging fellow Jamaicans to serve with dignity and urging that on no account should they let the Jamaican side down.

On reflection, Mr. King concluded how pathetic it is to see in Britain racists and their bedfellows harassing minorities. The world today is a very different place to what it was then, and make no mistake as to what it would be like if that struggle had been lost. Society may appear to forget the ex-servicemen and women's heroic fighting spirit, for which we owe a priceless debt of gratitude.

Mr Gardner remembered too that they were boys who became men overnight. He noted that West Indians were welcomed on their arrival in Britain throughout the war. It was an encouraging experience to observe people of different nationalities living and working together in harmony.

Mr. Gardner observed how European men differed in their own environment to their kin in the colonies. Nevertheless, he was disappointed that Caribbeans were asked so many ill-conceived questions about their lifestyles. Mr. Garner testifies, too, to the sharpness, even now, of memories from that time.

Mr. Goulbourne recalled that he had refused to join the police force as a prelude to the army. Some ninety volunteers, excluding the RAF men, were from Jamaica. Goulbourne was transferred to the REME, from whence they were split up and sent to different parts of the country. He was detailed to guard German prisoners-of-war and countered one of the prisoners questions as to why he was fighting for Britain, pointing out what Owens and Joe Louis had done to the pride of the Nazi so-called 'Master Race'. It is for that reason that when he saw the National Front marching with the Union Jack, he was convinced that the prisoner might have had a point.

Wartime service was not all fighting and seriousness as Mr. Newtown Palmer related. An evening of entertainment, which he attended, went so well that he missed the last bus and was misdirected to another camp further away. He was fortunate to return without being noticed and fell asleep, missing the morning parade. Palmer awoke to find the sergeant standing over him. He was given a thorough lesson about military discipline and sent to the back of the class.

Caribbean citizens who served in the Navy, Army and the RAF, suffered casualties. A Royal Air Force pilot, Joseph, for example, was shot down on New Year's Eve 1944 during the 'Battle of the Bulge' when the war was almost won. As far as the native English community was concerned, the best-known Caribbean fatality was not a serviceman but entertainer Ken 'Snakeships' Johnson who was killed when a bomb fell on the Cafe Royal ballroom. After hostilities ceased, service personnel returned home with the horizons of their vision extended.

Barbadian Winston Hyman, the former secretary warden of the West Indian Students Centre, arrived in Britain during the war and served in the RAF Bomber Command for seven years. He was awarded both the Distinguished Flying Medal and the Distinguished Flying Cross. He was later involved in social work. He became a member of the British Legion, as well as the Transport Salaried Staff Association. He believed that by not voting in sufficient numbers the African-Caribbean community of the 1960s had not taken advantage of its political potential.

Theo Campbell, a pioneer of West Indian journalism in Britain, found also that his work with the youth was derived from the experiences of his RAF days. He was a member of the Liberal party Immigration Panel, joint-Treasurer of the British Caribbean Association, and a founder of the Jamaican Overseas Families & Friends Association. He is reported as saying that we are a well integrated community in the Caribbean and we must fight for integration in the United Kingdom. Campbell had close contacts with West Indian cricketers living in Britain during the war. Among them was Bertie Clarke, whose number also included Sgt. E.A. Williams.

Sam Morris was in the army for 22 years. He took over from Sir John Carter as General Secretary of the League of Coloured Peoples, and was assistant to Lord Learie Constantine at the Welfare Department of the Colonial Office. After being press officer to President Kwame Nkrumah of Ghana for eight years, Morris returned to Britain in 1967. The following year he became Deputy Chief Officer of the Community Relations Council. He travelled throughout the country promoting better understanding and espousing the hope that West Indians would take advantage of available opportunities to better themselves. The Sam Morris Society - an exhibition centre in Hackney, has been named after Morris .

From a later generation, Rudolph Aaron, President of the West Indian Students Union, spent four years with the army in Germany, six months in East Africa, and one year in Northern Island. Trinidadian-born Flight Sergeant Percy Lewis became one of Britain's best known airmen in the 1950s by representing the country in international amateur boxing competitions, including the Olympic Games. Later, he won the professional Commonwealth featherweight title. He was an exceptional boxing stylist, without a particularly heavy punch. Lewis was a fine amateur but could not get past Hogan Bassey in paid contests.

The early immigrants did not join the police force because they had only a temporary presence in Britain. Even after the Notting Hill riots confirmed that the community needed protection from extreme elements, few ventured to be 'bobbies' on the beat. It was inevitable that an adversarial relationship (them and us) would ensue, considering reported heated exchanges between former service men and the police. Failure in making a real effort to recruit men and women into the police force, once it was seen that the black community was here to stay, lacked vision on the part of the Home Office. This strategy would have aided confidence building like nothing else could.

Constable Norwell Roberts at Bow Street police station was one of the first to be recruited at age 21. He was born in Anguilla. He studied at the Paddington Technical Institute and worked previously as a laboratory technician at the University of London. PC Roberts enjoyed cricket, basketball, rugby football, boxing, squash, table tennis, and football. He regretted that more West Indians were not in the force. Young people were reluctant to join for two principal reasons; firstly, their community was not represented in the hierarchy and secondly, promotional prospects were exceedingly low for African-Caribbean officers.

Opinion varies as to whether the appointment of black policemen/women should be publicised to attract other recruits from the community or whether that would constitute unnecessary trivia. Perhaps the majority of newcomers tend to hold the latter view, but the West Midlands found a way to resolve this anomaly by offering WPC Marcia Clarke a prominent role in general recruitment.

Engaging the community in all aspects of national life advances that sense of belonging, removing doubts and fear. The ethnic mix, for example, in popular television serials such as *The Bill, London's Burning* and *Casualty*, has shown the importance of bridge building through recruitment practices in the Police and Fire Services respectively.

Loosely organised community-based groups, either through individual initiatives or through organisations such as WISC, and established consultative links with the police in their area. This practise of liaison building became more standardised with the development of the professional community relations industry. Entry into community relations work first, or with a local authority agency, often led to association with the police and a possible career in the force. Some senior officers, who were aware of the importance of racial harmony, have been regular guests at various African-Caribbean community events.

Mrs. Hyacinth Moodie served as a comparatively early member of the liaison committee between the police and the community. She was welfare officer for WISC and the Association of Jamaicans, a member of the Royal College of Midwives and the Walthamstow Community Relations Council, amongst other organisations. She believed that parents should be responsible for the general welfare of their children. In 1977 she received the Badge of Honour for meritorious service (Jamaica), the Caribbean Times Award (1986) and in that same year, the Asian Artist Award from Watlham Forest.

The Brockley International Friendship Association in Lewisham was probably the most dynamic of those associated with WISC in building police community relations.

Events leading to the inner-city disturbances of 1981 widened the rift between the black youth and the police. It was the culmination of discontent which saw the introduction of Special Patrol Groups and the stop-and-search campaign. Clashes between young people and the police were publicised extensively, especially during the Notting Hill Carnival. The provocative marches by the National Front in the late 1970s, coupled with the police action, showed how insensitive sections of the British population were to the needs of the black community.

So ingrained is the African-Caribbean community's distrust of the police, that victims of crime were reluctant to seek redress. The failure of the authorities to take appropriate action in cases involving miscarriages of justice (such as the racial killing of 18 year old student Stephen Lawrence in 1993) or deaths in police custody might be easily explained to the bureaucratic mind, but it does nothing to restore public confidence. Antagonism was a potent force in the aftermath of the fire, which killed a number of black people at a party in New Cross, South London, in January 1981. This incident was virtually a time bomb ticking way - only awaiting human ignition to explode.

In 1969, twelve years before the racial disturbances broke out in the Handsworth district of Birmingham, the former Director of Education in Hackney, Gus John, reported to the Runnymede Trust on the tension existing between black people and the police. His was not a lone voice. Four years later, John Biggs-Davidson, a Conservative MP, warned about the probability of similar disturbances in Brixton and Birmingham. The younger generation, having been made aware of their birth rights, unlike their parents, were not as acquiescent and complacent. In this intense atmosphere, the extensive recruitment of police officers in the black community had little effect on the state of race relations.

The experiences of the early 1980s brought to prominence several committed, if not self-appointed, spokespersons for the black community, campaigning for justice and fairplay. Barrister Rudy Narayan served for a time as a Lambeth councillor. He was involved in some significant cases, and founded the Society of Black Lawyers and spearheaded the foundation of Black Rights (UK). The Guyanese possessed a rare talent in oratory. His charmed offensive as a champion of the unjust gave him instant popularity. His book 'Barrister for the Defence' gave a critical account of his experiences with the criminal justice system and his own thoughts on the adversarial nature of the judiciary, a view shared by staunch advocates of the British legal system.

Trinidadian Darcus Howe became known after defending himself successfully in the 1970 Mangrove Nine trial. Four years on, he became editor of Race Today. As far as the national press was concerned he was a leading spokesman (in popular agitation) following the New Cross debacle. Since 1985 he has been associated with the Bandung File, a television programme for the African-Caribbean and Asian communities, which he founded with Tariq Ali. The Devil's Advocate, which began in the early 1990s, was another outstanding television programme initiative founded by Howe in an effort to allow public officials to account for their actions in the black community.

The importance of law and order and police-related activities were seen by the high profile accorded to Paul Boateng, a former Greater London Councillor, who chaired the GLC Police Committee. A solicitor by profession, he represented families in Brixton and Broadwater Farm during the disturbances there. He was among the first group of black MPs to be elected in 1987. In 1989 he became the first black politician to be promoted to the Front Bench of the Labour Party. A Londoner by birth, he has a strong voice for the Black British political aspirations. On May 1, 1997, he became the first black government minister to be appointed. Boateng is currently Chief Secretary to the Treasury in the Labour Government.

The sense of optimism contained in the proposals introduced by Lord Scarman's report was soon evaporated by two events in 1985; namely, the shooting of Cherry Groce (which left her paralysed) in Brixton and Cynthia Jarrett's death while officers were vigorously searching her home in Tottenham. The latter fuelled the Broadwater Farm riot which resulted in PC Blakelock's death. This was indeed the low point in relations between the police and the black community. This period of acrimony aroused even greater suspicion and fear of attacks from both sides.

Jeff Crawford, who was born in Barbados, served on the Police Complaints Board and was involved in several cases mostly affecting the African-Caribbean community. He has participated in community relations overall since coming to the United Kingdom in the late 1950s. His outspokeness and frequent press gained him much respect as secretary of WISC in the momentous years - 1963 to 1970. He was chairman of the North London West Indian Association and founder of the Caribbean Workshop.

The first edition of Westindians in Great Britain (1973/74) reported that Crawford has done more to highlight the shortcomings of our society than anyone else we knew. In almost twenty years since holding several offices, it is likely that Jeff Crawford will be present at events that are important to society. He has demonstrated the necessity for African-Caribbean people's participation and general involvement in local and national decision-making processes.

While the example of influential persons are vital, it is community involvement in all areas that will make the difference between success and failure in the years to come. I have been encouraged by the recruitment drive introduced by the Police Commissioner for officers from all the ethnic communities. Young ambitious African-Caribbean people with encouragement are now taking up positions in the armed services - the army, the navy and the air force. Some have participated in military action in the Falklands, Northern Ireland, as well as with NATO forces in West Germany.

There has been some distressing news recently of intolerable racial harassment of black recruits in the prestige guard regiments - though it is tempting to surmise that a degree of brutality may be inevitable anyway (if the film 'The Bofors Gun' had a bearing of truth) - those involved with military service experience are better equipped for a profession after demobilisation.

During the Second World War, American servicemen were segregated racially, but their British counterparts were not, which signals mutual respect as each other's keeper in the face of danger.

Patriotism for the United Kingdom runs high in the Caribbean, so that it was natural to volunteer the services of the region.

Building goodwill and trust in our mutual national interest calls for a resolute will by all concerned in the strengthening of a more cohesive society.

The Historical and International Context

The success of Black enterprise development should not be limited to the British Isles. By necessity, it is influenced by the overall tradition of African-Caribbean people who achieved much before, during and after subsequent periods of physical enslavement and colonialism. It will be recalled that prior to the invasion of Africa and the consequential displacement of African society, our ancestors administered and controlled their own resources - through a vibrant commercial and industrial trading system. While a sense of history is important towards a proper understanding of our achievements as a race, such facts tend to have little application in the present context of economic and social change which has created a situation of depression.

Therefore, it is important to have contemporary figures with whom we can identify. We need to see more successful men and women who have risen from obscurity, and who by their own efforts, have succeeded. In previous chapters, I have looked at the number of African-Caribbean people and Africans who have made the transition in our community in Britain. In this chapter, their achievements will be placed in an international context. In the 1950s, there was a popular book for boys in primary schools called 'Daring Deeds Which Won The Empire', which presented a picture of commitment, dedication and self-sacrifice.

There is a dearth of similar literature describing such noble qualities of those on the receiving end. Yet these very attributes have characterised our resilience and general survival in times of despair. It is hoped that succeeding generations will build on the legacy of achievements bequeathed to them by our parents, our children and us. The lack of adequate outlets and in some instances, inappropriate information channels, has resulted in either a distortion or a diminishing of the real impact African-Caribbean people have on universal progress.

The achievements of the West Indian cricket team are entirely due to solid support from our community. As a credible regional institution, cricket provides a forum for the celebration of parity and pride. While the African-Caribbean community in Britain is not particularly fond of cricket as gleaned from the sparse attendance at matches, Test series have elevated our status as a proud people, in the lyrics of Jimmy Cliff 'higher-heights'.

The late political authors - Trinidadian C.L.R. James and Jamaican

153

Michael Norman Manley - wrote authoritatively on the game. James' 'Beyond the Boundary' and Manley's 'History of West Indies Cricket' are seminal works which demonstrate the importance of this artistic enterprise to every Caribbean man, woman and child. Unlike a generation ago, West Indian cricket has transcended class, colour, creed and race. Many players from humble beginnings have reaped substantial rewards and in the process, have enhanced their social status. Young West Indian players continue to point to the importance of seizing opportunities in niche markets, through applied creativity, daring enterprise and honed intelligence.

So then, where did it all start? Did the Europeans bring civilisation to Africa? Did Africans accept slavery without opposition? I will discuss some of these questions in this chapter, by showing how we adapted to profound changes in our political, economic and social environment. It was however, through the talent and dedication of many that some of our stalwarts achieved recognition and brought success to our community. Let me therefore start at the beginning.

African civilisations have existed since the dawn of history. It is a truism that Mankind began on the continent. The Egyptian Empire was the first, and in many ways the greatest, continuous civilisation. It all seems so long ago today. We should remember that when European scholars refer to the exploits of Cleopatra, her existence is a thousand years apart from the Pharaohs who built the pyramids of Egypt. In fact Christianity has been around for only two thousand years, but the Egyptian Empire lasted for three millennia. It did not end there however.

A series of merchant empires existed in West Africa from about 700 to 1800 A.D. The Ghana Empire, to the north-west of the present state of that name, flourished between 700 and 1200. It was absorbed and extended westwards by Mali for another three centuries. Songhai developed slowly from 1350 and gradually took over Mali until it, too, passed into history. Kanem-Bornu was several hundred miles separated from the others in the interior of the continent and lasted a thousand years from about 800. All had individual characteristics and achieved standards of performance which would surprise those who believe in the misleading term 'Dark Continent'.

An organised system of commerce was in place, linking trading centres with inland regions and the coast. One Portuguese scribe observed:

"In this land there are rich merchants, and there is much gold and silver and amber and musk and pearls. Those of the land wear clothes of fine cotton and of silk and many fine things, and they are black men."

These cities included Kilwa, Mombassa, Malindi, Kisimani-Mafia and Mogadishu. A Zimbabwe empire rose to power in 1440, and was known as the Monomotapa Empire after the honorary title of its rulers, and the imperial rule was extended by the Rozwi dynasty who raised the Great Temple of Zimbabwe.

When the great trade routes broke down, new kingdoms became known in the forests of the Congo and what is now Nigeria. These areas were severely affected by slave raids. The historically famous Ashanti kingdom possessed the finest mercantile traders of that era immediately prior to European colonisation. The Ashantis were well schooled in commerce and diplomacy and they employed these skills diligently to keep both the British and the Dutch at bay. Even so, their riches attracted predators, and the British broke their power in 1901 in what was known as a devastating colonial war.

Benin was an even greater power with a strong monarchy and thriving commerce. Although this civilisation shared in the flowering of African art, it was more martial than usual. It was eventually weakened by war. Benin sent an ambassador to Portugal at the turn of the 15th century. He was described as "a man of good speech and natural wisdom." The Yoruba kingdom, too, was shaped by fighting its neighbour but had little resources to repel the Europeans. Thus, the flames of European domination at the beginning of the 20th century doused complete West African independence.

The Africans who were taken to the Caribbean and North America as slaves did not always accept their lot without opposition. Although it was not possible to organise widespread uprisings, due to the poor state of communications at the time and because power lay in the hands of imperial administrators, the history of the region is rich with examples of slave revolts, which attained varying degrees of success. Transportation destroyed former social and national groupings, but the Europeans had given the slaves an important new weapon in their struggle for emancipation - the Bible.

The slaves read and interpreted Christ's salvation unto them. In accepting the Holy Word literally, they saw the exile of the Israelites in Egypt and Babylon an apt parallel with their own experience. Preachers were in the forefront of the liberation struggle. Samuel Sharpe was a leader in the Baptist Church in Jamaica. He persuaded slaves not to return to their plantations. The disturbance was suppressed with much bloodshed. Some Africans did return to Africa. The Americans returned some of the most rebellious, and most difficult to control, to Sierra Leone, and freed slaves set up their own state in Liberia.

The 1789 uprising in the French colony of St. Domingue (today known as Haiti) reverberated throughout the Caribbean region and the America in general. The great soldier and statesman, Toussaint L'Ouverture, Jean-Jacques Dessalines and Henri Christophe, all proved themselves capable of leading the island, repelling attempts by Europeans to regain control. A new state was thus established. Subsequent divisions arose due to inexperience and differences on the part of leaders. At one stage also, England comprised seven or more different kingdoms. It took centuries to bring about the Union with Northern Ireland, Scotland and Wales.

The most famous slave rebellion occurred at Morant Bay in Jamaica in 1865. The hatred was directed against the island's colonial government and the plantocracy. Deacon Paul Bogle and George William Gordon, who later became Jamaican national heroes, were killed in the aftermath of the rebellion. The failure of the Morant Bay conflict extinguished for several generations the hope of taking over, or even influencing the administration by direct action. In any case, since emancipation, the African-Caribbean population have directed their energies towards political independence and self-government.

Regaining the economic foothold is a key to the salvation of the African-Caribbean community. Our ancestors' struggle has always been linked to spiritual consciousness and renewal. Africans understood that Christianity in Egypt and Ethiopia had a longer tradition compared to the greater part of Western Europe. As far as Ethiopia was concerned, there was a symbolic relationship with the sole independent African state which resisted the Europeans and had defeated the Italians at Adowa in 1896. American-born George Liele went to Jamaica and founded the Ethiopian Baptist Church in 1784. This denomination had a considerable following in the latter part of the 19th century.

Marcus Mosiah Garvey was born in Jamaica in 1887 on the eve of the African independent struggle. Hailed as the 'Father of Pan-Africanism', although this doctrine existed before his time, he nevertheless gave it new meaning to the political and intellectual world. He travelled extensively and established the universal Negro Improvement Association, which had a large membership, when he moved to the US. His exhortations of self-government, self-help and group power appealed to the Black Diaspora worldwide, especially in places where cruel injustices were meted out against black people. His economic project ,the Black Starline, was intended to be used as a vessel to transport produce between the industrialised and non-industrialised world. This venture collapsed due to poor management experience and unscrupulous supporters, coupled by an unjust system which disfavoured black economic power.

Garvey was deported to Jamaica in the late 1920s and he later moved to England where he died in 1940. His 'Back to Africa 1' call drew strength from Ethiopia, being boosted by the enthronement of Emperor Haile Selassie in 1930 and the parallel Ras Tafari movement. The movements sharing that view called themselves 'Rastafaris' and acknowledged the divinity of the emperor. Since Italy's invasion of Ethiopia in the mid-1930s, sharp divisions have taken place between Europeans and Africans.

Two years prior to that period, the brilliant American sociologist, author and political activist, William. E. B. DuBois, resigned from the National Association for the Advancement of Coloured People (NAACP) in America. Almost three decades earlier, he had founded the forerunner movement of the Association in opposition to what he perceived as Booker T. Washington's accommodation with white supremacy. An outstanding scholar, Du Bois had enormous influence on those who shaped world affairs in the next generation. He spent the last months of his life in Ghana. He was a loyal compatriot of the late President of Ghana, and another Pan-Africanist, Dr. Kwame Nkrumah.

Dr. Martin Luther King Jr., had a major influence on our generation. The reawakening of our cultural consciousness following the Notting Hill disturbance in 1958 reflected a scale similar to historic events in the US. School integration in the southern states, such as Little Rock, and civil unrest created a world media focus for the first time on the American black community. King's exemplary role in the campaign to end segregation on the buses in Montgomery, Mississippi, propelled him to the leadership of the Civil Rights Movement. Here was the case of a man meeting the hour.

Dr. King was a young and brilliant orator, and had the twin advantages of being both non-violent and successful. His sincerity of purpose resulted in frequent imprisonment and sectional hatred for his belief in, and value of, the human spirit. More than anything else, he demonstrated that black people, who so frequently fragmented and turned against each other, could organise an effective mass movement. At the start of the 1960s many West Indian families in Britain displayed photographs of President Kennedy in appreciation for his contribution to the prevailing spirit of liberation, but those of King replaced these. Both men subsequently died by the bullet.

The high point of King's career however, was the Great March on Washington on 28th August 1963 involving 200,000 people. Although he was honoured with the Nobel Peace Prize the following year, he was overtaken by the repercussions of his own success. Malcolm X superseded Elijah Muhammad in the leadership of the Black Muslim movement, and offered an alternative philosophy in which segregation would replace integration.

King's involvement in the wider political sphere, especially in his opposition to the American participation in the Vietnam conflict, meant that he was prepared to adopt a greater role as a universal peace ambassador rather than the restricted theme of Civil Rights in one country. This recognition heralded a new development in the black liberation struggle worldwide. He was still under forty years old when he was shot on the balcony of his hotel in Memphis, Tennessee - 4th April 1968. The formation of short-term, but seemingly sustainable foundation schemes in various countries, are testament to his unique role and his contribution to history, which is fittingly commemorated by the annual Martin Luther King Day in the US on the 13th January.

You only have to contrast the role of the African-Caribbean community in the US before King's public career to the time of his assassination to understand the impact he had and still has. A similar process unfolded in other societies globally. Dr. King himself was influenced by the non-violent doctrine of Indian-born Mahatma Mohandas Karamchand Gandhi who co-ordinated opposition to British rule in India, leading the way for Home Rule (political independence) and thereby setting a precedent which was spread to almost every part of the former imperial domain. India in fact is today's largest democracy on earth.

While both Dr. King's and Malcolm X's struggle impacted much on the ideological and political equation, the economic dimension of their philosophy should not be forgotten. It is through their consistency of views in this area, that they appealed to the consciousness of both the African Diaspora and liberal whites the world over. Today, much of their work is germane to the formulation of strategies aimed at countering the current inequities of the global political and social order.

Muhammed Ali (former Cassius Clay) assumed a model assertive role, becoming in the process, a dynamic larger-than-life personality. Ali was more than just a pure boxer-athlete and showman. Those who criticised his frequent showmanship and the frequent question, "what's my name" to opponents who dared to use his former name, missed the point in both a historical and social context. Unlike his predecessors, despite fame and glory, Ali was fiercely proud of his race - a fact which critics never understood nor appreciated - both in and out of the boxing ring. He led the cause of his community. By his own example, he proved that business success should be matched by social responsibility.

Some of his predecessors had contrasting outlooks: Floyd Patterson for instance, was apologetic and inward looking; Sonny Liston, scowling and anti-social, while the unknown Ezzard Charles lacked personality and was unknown. Perhaps only Sugar Ray Robinson demonstrated an Ali-like style and a knack for communication. The 'Louisville Lip' as he was sometimes described, was known to millions of people, who otherwise would not have been interested in the 'Manly Art' (boxing). Those champions preceding him were appendages to the system. After him, however, African-Caribbean people were represented at all levels of pugilism, including administration, management, marketing and promotion.

Because of their high profile, sportsmen and women have enhanced their public image in the world. The 1930s were blessed with black sports personalities in various departments: athletes, boxers and cricketers, with exceptional talent and character. Joe Louis, Jesse Owens and George Headley (nicknamed the Black Bradman, the equivalent of the Australian post-war batsman, Sir Donald Bradman) were all cast in this rare mould.

Interestingly also, is the irrepressible power with which black entertainers opened the doors into white homes through their voices on records and films. Even those who were not usually so well disposed to us as a people, were impressed by the ranging subtlety and finesse of musical greats: Scott Joplin, Duke Ellington, Count Basey, Ella Fitzgerald, Dizze Gillespie, Nat King Cole and Miles Davis. Then to add the tantalising sounds of Lena Horne, Aretha Franklin, Tina Turner, Dionne Warwick and her cousin, Whitney Houston. Group singers now legendary include the Platters, the Drifters, the Supremes the Pointer Sisters and the Osmonds, while artistes like Michael Jackson and Diana Ross have revolutionised lyrical compositions and presentations. Other genres include calypsos, socca, and reggae, to name but a few. Harry Belafonte was one of the biggest stars on screen in the 1950s, and Bahamian-born Sidney Poiter became a screen hero in the next decade. Films such as 'Guess Who's

Coming To Dinner' and 'Island In The Sun', converted racial tolerance into a virtue and victimisation, a vice. Yet this was a glossy make-believe world. Reality was so much different.

Black artists wove threads of realism through their literature as is the case of the African American James Baldwin. He broke through the racial barrier with a sequence of uncompromising novels, including 'Another Country', 'Go Tell It On The Mountain' and 'Giovanni's Room'. His 'Fire Next Time' was a more straightforward statement of belief and observation.

The rich cultural mix of music, sports and entertainment, encouraged black people, in the 1960s in particular, to search more thoroughly into their own history and culture.

Naturally, Africa has always held an especial interest for generations. When the Second World War ended, the British, French and the Dutch still had much of Africa, Asia and the West Indies as their colonial possessions, in spite of military defeats by the Japanese. The tide of history had turned, however, and some of the Pan-African ideas, which were discussed previously came to fruition. The Gold Coast of Ghana was the first African country to achieve political independence in 1957.

Dr. Kwame Nkrumah, who served as Prime Minister and later President, was a noted student of Marcus Garvey's work and himself the author of 'Towards Colonial Freedom' by the time he became general secretary of the United Gold Coast Convention in the late 1940s. He was imprisoned for his part in organising politically-motivated riots, but was released when elections made him the country's leader-in-waiting. Nkrumah played a leading role in the Organisation of African Unity (which was established in 1963). By the time he was ousted by a military coup, former European colonies on the continent gained self- rule.

In east Africa, the clash between the Mau Mau movement and the administrators in the early 1950s ignited the situation in Kenya. That country too found a universally accepted leader, Jomo Kenyatta, who commanded both the respect and loyalty of the nation. He was imprisoned on suspicion of involvement in the Mau Mau, but retained his position of leadership. Kenya gained independence peacefully in 1964. Doctors Julius Nyerere (Tanzania) and Kenneth Kaunda (Zambia) , both proven leaders, led their countries on similar paths.

South Africa was becoming increasingly isolated, and although that country had never been a good example of racial harmony, the electoral victory of the National Party in 1948 led directly to the official imposition of Apartheid - a legally enforced system of racial segregation and disadvantage. Over the years the government tightened its grip, and opposition was made difficult because of the size of the country and the complexity of different ethnic and social groups within its borders. All the same, there emerged leaders of great international repute to challenge this hideous system.

Albert John Luthuli, a traditional chief, was awarded the Nobel Peace Prize for his peaceful struggle against apartheid. He was born in 1898 and 54 years later became president of the African National Congress (ANC) until the government banned it. Luthuli suffered the banning and harassment, which his contemporaries and successors have shared. It was this action in 1960 which resulted in some members losing faith in the efficacy of non-violence and instead reverting to direct protest action. With the emergence of Nelson Mandela, the rules of political engagement changed considerably. In effect, Mandela became the symbol of opposition against white supremacy in South Africa. Luthuli was struck by a train and died 1967. In the first multi-racial elections held in South Africa 1994, Mandela's ANC was swept to power with a majority.

Against the backdrop of these events and more, the fight for political independence intensified in the West Indies. In 1958 the West Indies Federation was set up with the support of the most powerful politicians in the region - Norman Manley of Jamaica, Dr. Eric Williams of Trinidad, T. A. Marryshow of Grenada and Sir Grantley Adams of Barbados. It seemed that harmony would continue after the achievement of independence, but this was not to be so. Passionate national interests replaced unity. The Jamaican Labour Party, led by Sir Alexander Bustamante, was apprehensive that as the larger island it would have to bear the brunt of the cost.

He won a national referendum on this issue, and the ensuing election. With Jamaica leaving the Federation, the next biggest island territory, Trinidad, followed and the concept of regional integration was crippled. Political events in the Caribbean as such did not have a direct bearing on the African-Caribbean community in the United Kingdom, except to prevent the development of a regional figurehead to inspire the confidence and loyalty of all. The youth, born and raised in Britain without parochial loyalties, needed to find their heroes in activities outside of West Indian politics, whether it was in the political life abroad or in sport and entertainment.

The late Emperor and leader of Ethiopia, Haile Selassie, has proved one focal point of loyalty on the basis of Africentric cultural history. However, his Eminence is not altogether accepted by even a majority of Jamaicans, where Rastafarianism is strongest and most popular. The recent journey to Ethiopia by Ras Tafari, a black British poet from Liverpool, revealed the mixed reaction many have of the Selassie creed and legacy. The late Bob Marley's mystical lyrics on the 'Back to Africa' message are yet to be properly analysed and studied in the context of present day Africa and changes in the global superstructure.

In Britain, we don't have a Martin Luther King equivalent, in spite of the relentless efforts on the part of the national media to nominate a 'Black Leader' who can fit the bill. Such a development has to emerge through a gradual process of dialogue, discussion and mass education - an imposition of any sort will be counter-productive.

Talking in the broadest historical terms, African American and European Americans arrived in their respective homelands around the same time. Although they possess distinct cultures, they have each made an invaluable contribution to a new society. The 'Back to Africa' doctrine aside, the black American can ill-afford to be exiled elsewhere. He or she is more familiar with his or her territory and therefore, has to develop the country on that basis. The difference for West Indians however, is that they can chose to return to their former homelands which have a set structure and value system.

Thus the strong ties which reflect our local, regional and national identities, all have an impact on the way in which the African-Caribbean community sees itself as a racial or ethnic group in Britain. When the British-based West Indian community reads about the extraordinary gifts of Nelson Mandela and the wiles of Jesse Jackson and the prominence they are given in the black press, they feel less inclined to believe that Britain will ever possess such creditably distinguished leaders.

During the 1980s even the black newspapers manifested this trend with the West Indian World and the Jamaican Gleaner, losing substantial support to the more general African-Caribbean newspaper, the Voice. This of course was in the height of the election of the first group of black Members of Parliament, including the late Bernie Grant (Guyana), Dianne Abbot (Jamaica) and Paul Boateng (Ghana), with the late Grenadian Lord Pitt, the first black peer in the House of Lords. The latest crop of MPs are Oona King, Kumar Ashok, David Lammy, and Marsha Singh, while the Lords now include a further ten members.

Judging from the present situation, one should not assume that the black media in general, reflects a total Africentric view of African-Caribbean communities in Britain. It is hoped that with the presence of '*New Nation*', another black tabloid newspaper, there will be a move towards a balanced coverage and a truer reflection of the African-Caribbean community in the British Isles.

Against this background, little wonder Bob Marley, an all-embracing folk hero, has filled part of this identity gap. Reggae unites so many strands of sentiment. Marley grew up in the poorest township in Jamaica and became famous with the Wailers group (led by Bunny Wailer and the late Peter Tosh, all of whom were Marley's blood-brothers in the musical world) from the early 1960s. By 1975, he achieved superstardom. His career however was cut short by cancer and he succumbed to the disease in 1981 at age 37. His importance is measured by the quality of his achievements rather than by the years he lived. He has left a colossal legacy and a void in his musical repertoire that will be difficult to either replace or maintain.

A living monument to Marley's greatness is acknowledged by the world by his being voted artist of the millennium for his song "One Love".

Marley's espousal of Rastafarianism moved the creed into the mainstream of African-Caribbean thought. He represented every facet of the black community worldwide, whether within the African context at the Zimbabwean independence celebrations in 1980, or his well-attended multi-racial concerts in Western Europe, the United Kingdom and North America. He was in effect, a cultural ambassador cum peacemaker and unifier of all mankind. At a time when the political landscape in Jamaica appeared on the edge of electoral fratricide, Marley, alone, created a platform on which the leaders of both major political parties - the People's National Party (PNP, led by the late Michael Manley and the Jamaican Labour Party led by Edward Seaga, embraced a move unprecedented in the history of politics anywhere in the Caribbean. It is a lesson we need to savour in Britain as the African-Caribbean community continues contributing towards the development of a more cohesive society.

Raising The Stakes

Influencing change has to be, for the community, its number one consideration.

Reflecting on the past merely underlines a purposeful begining. The present evolves from the past and now we must look to the future and continue to build on the gains we have made. While there are no simple answers to achieving community success, from previous chapters it will be perfectly clear that the Afro Caribbean community has been making its solid contribution across British society. In some areas we carry the flag and actually lead the way in the case of sport. Names like Linford Christie, Lennox Lewis, Tessa Sanderson, Denise Lewis, Rio Ferdinand and Ian Wright are all world champions winning for Britain. We exercise our rights and responsibilities in equal measure and cannot be accused of being drones or passive onlookers.

The central community objective must be clear. We must work hard and play a meaningful role in the life of the nation. Despite the many handicaps experienced by unequal opportunity and racial discrimination, evidence of the strong desire to contribute, succeed and change our status is without doubt and is clearly demonstrable. There could not be a more positive note on which the black and ethnic contribution will continue to propel UK Plc forward.

What if these sterling efforts were strengthened by financial support, how much more would black creative talents have injected into the coffers of society?

A key issue in black community development is that the community itself must take on board the business of influencing and managing change in a similar way as the Jewish community has done, politically and financially.

This strategy calls for a committed sense of purpose, a dogged determination and an unshakable will to succeed.

The process must begin by taking a much greater interest in the political direction at the local level. We must begin by joining our local party organizations in our thousands which will send an unmistakable powerful message about our intentions.

Active membership will ensure that we are taken seriously, and our views taken into account. There is too much at stake in leaving our seats vacant around the table when our futures are discussed.

Exercising our political rights are vital elements in determining our destiny and our place in society in general. There can be little or no point of complaining or laying blame if we fail being part of the debating process of what happens in the town halls. Being present around the debating table is a precondition for black advancement and changing attitudes in society.

We must understand that as a community we cannot hope to improve our place in society by sitting on the fringe of it, we must for our salvation make our presence felt.

Among the ways of doing so is by becoming an effective force within the big political machine. Why is this so important? It is important because it gives us political leverage. Operation Black Vote statistical research has found that the Black vote currently holds the balance in 100 Parliamentary constituencies and can effectively determine which candidate goes to the House of Commons. This is real political power - the candidate is forced to take Black views into account!

The pursuit of economic strength goes hand in hand with political power. These are absolute essentials together with becoming a well-educated and informed community.

These are steps we must take for ourselves and for our children. Our whole socio-political status will always depend on our ability to sustain and maintain our basic interests at the end of the day as a community and part of the nation.

Simon Woolley, of *Operation Black Vote* reminds us, and I quote:-

"this is the tenth anniversary of the tragic death of Steven Lawrence, and despite huge efforts to address racism by many black people, particularly the Lawrence family, the problems that Black people face are as acute now as they were ten years ago."

Nevertheless, the legacy of the Lawrence family, which mirrors the Black struggle, is that in spite of tragedy we refuse to be defeated. The real prize that will effectively defeat racism is power: economic, political and spiritual power. Now more than ever the Black community must understand how these dynamics work and how we attain them.

The campaign in the battle for equal opportunity needs to be intensified working in alliances with all people of goodwill who endorse the principle of a multiracial society.

Here in Britain, we have a microcosm of the world at large and could showcase the merits of being one big international family whose mutual interests are inter-related and inter-dependent.

I have argued time and time over, that it is the denial of equal opportunity that makes us all the poorer as individuals and as a nation.

Evidence of unequal opportunity stares us in the face everywhere we look. Here in the UK, we have the largest numbers of university graduate mini car drivers, fast food servers, underground workers, petrol pump attendants and security guards, all working well below their qualifications, unable to make it into positions matching their abilities.

Not only is this situation soul-destroying, but let us consider for a moment the waste of expensively trained people unable to make a contribution relative to their abilities.

Many of the employers of the people in these jobs would tell you that they are "Equal Opportunity Employers" but yet the doors to middle or senior management remain firmly closed. The all-important element of "equal access" is missing and this is what keeps many of these graduates at the bottom of the pile, a situation that exists all over the place.

Building strong black business networks is one strategy that works and is a formidable tool, which must be brought into the frame. Its potential for building long term trading supplier / buyer partnerships, is a formula for complementary growth for both parties. Networking beyond the local and national market place through our international cultural links is a sure foundation for engaging in the rich emerging markets of the world.

Some years ago my company was invited by the British Overseas Trade Board to participate in a short film entitled "The World is Your Market" which was shown around the country, aimed at medium sized companies, stressing the added value exporting brings to a business. Every company with export potential must take on board the challenge of the export market place, which in most cases is usually more profitable and quite often incurs no additional overheads for the business.

A major handicap experienced by a large number of Afro-Caribbean businesses in the retail sector is the failure by its natural customer base to support and patronize businesses owned by their compatriots, even where they are competitive. This odd behaviour arises out of a belief that black shop-keepers are always more expensive, or given to cheating.

This behaviour pattern is a throw back from the days of slavery and indoctrination as it persists more so with the older generation of black shoppers who fail to understand the dynamics in building community economic structures. In some areas where the practice persists, where there is a choice of where to shop; the issue is often petty envy.

I recall an occasion when one of my good Jewish friends invited me out to lunch during the working day. Where are we going to lunch I enquired. Stamford Hill he said. That is a long way I interjected. Well, he retorted with a smile, "keeping the money in the family is so important", he explained.

Here is one lesson in community support that blacks need to learn and understand, that supporting young black businesses, where one legitimately can, represents an investment in helping to build the overall black community asset base.

Loyalty, my good friend, demonstrated, begins at home, and ends abroad. And why not. Every other community in Britain, apart from the Afro-Caribbean, practices this approach, the Jews, Asians, Greeks and others.

Consider the contrast of the young woman who was browsing in my store. There was no one else in the store at the time and I thought here was an opportunity to apply my luncheon friend's principle. I turned to her with what I hoped was a winning phrase, *"It was nice to see you keeping it in the family"* only to be promptly told that she "...was not going to help to make me rich." When will we learn? There is also, on the other hand, the endemic question of trust and individualism rather than pooling resources to tackle large scale projects.

Some possible solutions in helping to bridge the gap in community influence, could well begin by a more in depth engagement in all areas of civic society.

Critical elements in advancing change, requires active participation on some of the following local authority key committees as stake holders. Serving as school governors, sitting on education boards, Hospital Health Trusts, Community Health Councils, becoming police liaison officers, being active tenant association committee members, getting involved in local environmental and leisure committees and others.

The high incidence of poor under-achievement at school for black boys, for example, could well be the lack of parental involvement in their children's welfare in their early school years, where moulding of their character begins. Failure in this department leads to low aspirations, a clear route to insecurity and a resultant culture of crime. This is an area for urgent community attention. There must be no hiding place for criminals in the community. This small destructive minority, damages and destroys the huge efforts of the majority of law abiding citizens. In the delicate area of police relations and black youth, we must together work extra hard to bring about a more just, and a more harmonious society. Getting these issues right are cornerstones in building the kind of society to which we all aspire.

Turning now to the problem of community businesses. Accessing bank finance remains by far the major barrier between start up, stagnation and preventing young black progressive men and women from leaping forward.

Nick Mathiason, in his article on business focus/financial regeneration in the Observer of 9th March 2003, coins a phrase, "*CUSTOMERS OF NO ACCOUNT*" . He slams the banks. In the article Mathiason states, and I quote *"British banks are betraying the poor"* and substantiates his case by quoting the British Bankers Association own report of September 2002 which shows that for black start-up entrepreneurs, one in five secured backing against one in three for white start-ups.

British banks must wake up to their corporate responsibility in this regard. They need no reminding that they earn and hold hundreds of millions by way of investment and savings from within the black communities and reinvesting some of their earnings in the community will at the end of the day further swell their huge reserves.

The African-Caribbean Business Network and other similar organisations carry a heavy responsibility in shaping and influencing the future role of enterprise in Britain. The membership needs no reminding of the benefits that a strong and respected body can command. But like everything else, it must earn that respect.

Drawing on my experience I want to warn of an inherent danger, which somehow seems to be ever present in our community organisations, one which we must contain and rise above. Meetings, in the first place, lack the first rule of discipline, which leads to disorder and disruption detracting from the business in hand.

Failure to unite behind the leadership and jockeying for positions undermines and destroys the organisation. A case in point was the UK Caribbean Chamber of Commerce. The Chamber was painstakingly built, delivering practical support to emerging businesses, and in the process had earned national respect at all levels of government and across society generally.

With myself as chairman and Colin Carter as secretary, the organisation had matured to a point where we were in well advanced discussions with government to separate the chamber functions and build a government sponsored business development arm to further assist our many small businesses.

Agreement in principle was reached in the week prior to the chamber's AGM and final discussions with the Home Office were put on hold till after the election. It was with great sadness that I had to report to the Home Office the election was lost by the entire office holders. The government withdrew from the project and the community lost a golden opportunity.

It is well worth mentioning how the coup was engineered. In an effort to expand the organisation, a membership drive was launched, and as it happened, at the last meeting before the election, seventeen new members were introduced. Contrary to the usual practice of vetting the applications, these were all accepted *en bloc* and played into the hands of the plotter, who literally hijacked the Chamber which self destructed in a matter of months.

The really big hurt was to witness the destruction of years of hard work and effort destroyed by a handful of bandits in a matter of months, an act that has set the business community back by an estimated fifty years. The above is a lesson for us all and the reason for my caution.

Equal opportunity remains my passion and my vision is that hopefully, the dawning of a truly inclusive society is not far off. Our banks could very well take a lead in helping ethnic people in opening markets for our goods and services in the emerging markets around the world. It is no secret that the ethnic appetite for doing just that exists. And the fuel for oiling it rests with the banks.

Having said that, some other ethnic groups have their own banks and there is no reason why black business leadership should not look at this possibility. An invitation to Shore Bank of Chicago, the largest community bank in the world, to manage such an institution would be music to their ears. It started life some thirty years ago in one of the poorest areas in Chicago and today operates in Europe, Africa and parts of Asia. Its success formula has been staying close to its customers with guidance and direction. It has been reported that Shore Bank has one of the highest returns on capital with bad debts well below the average.

Change is not a one sided matter. The question of putting black Britons to work more effectively is a matter of urgent concern for the whole nation. Employment opportunities for the growing numbers of black school leavers, raises economic, social and political questions which require bold new initiatives.

The Secretary of State for Trade and Industry, Patricia Hewitt, must be congratulated for her positive comments reported in the Weekly Gleaner 12/18th March 2003. *"The new data shows that people from ethnic minority communities make a large and important contribution to the entrepreneurial spirit of our country"* she said. She continued. *"This finding is particularly welcome. Our role as Government must be to ensure that individuals from minority backgrounds who want to start their own businesses are supported in doing so".*

How many times have the ethnic communities heard these sound bites? Hopefully this time round the Secretary of State will deliver on government promises, but now it is a question of wait and see.

A catalogue of promises leaves the black community to question the

Secretary of State's bold statement.

The 1977 Government White Paper Policy statement for the inner cities stated, *"minority groups living in the inner areas need to be given full opportunity to play their part in the task of regeneration"*.

Six years later, October 1983, the Financial Guardian investigated the outcome of the 1977 policy statement. Its headline on the subject read, *"minorities find the climate cold and bleak"*.

Peter Wilson of the London Business School carried out the research. His findings were as follows:

"Constraints on access to finance, including difficulties with banks, constraints in the physical environment, including access to premises together with disadvantages imposed by racial discrimination, all combine to hold back the community".

Two years later, the Labour force survey published by the Department of Employment found that blacks face twice the employment rate of whites.

While there have been some attempts by government policies to address the problems of unequal opportunities, these have been frustrated in many cases at the point of delivery. A report was carried out on behalf of the UK Caribbean Chamber of Commerce by Aston University, Birmingham, and Consultant Martin Kazuka. They reported as follows:

" The purpose of the Inner Urban Areas Act 1978, was to help inner urban areas by economic regeneration through a mixture of central and local government funding, to help increase employment opportunities in designated areas. Hackney, where the Chamber was based, was one such area.

Department of Environment circular number 269/78 gave the guidance to local authorities under which the loan and grant applications were considered. It is clear from analysis that most Black and Asian businesses would qualify under the Act because most of them were in retail trading. Its provisions however did not cover shops and services.

This was a disturbing situation because the provisions appear to discriminate against Black and Asian businesses because none of them represented industrial or commercial companies. It could be argued, very plausibly, that the effect of the DOE circular 1969/78 was unintentionally discriminatory in a racial sense, in that if its guidelines were to be followed to the letter, no Black, nor the majority of Asian businesses would have benefited from the Act, because none of them belonged to the industrial and commercial categories specified by the Act."

Similarly, the Small Firms Assistance Bill did nothing for ethnic minority businesses and prospective entrepreneurs to enter business since it did not contain any specific provisions directed at them." The Loans Guarantee Scheme was well intentioned, but here again the banks rendered it useless by refusing to apply it, especially when dealing with non-white firms.

Seventeen years on, September 2002, a Financial Times headline written by Jonathan Guthrie read, "Banks tougher on black start-ups, Afro-Caribbean entrepreneurs face greater problems than other ethnic groups in raising finance." This was a Department of Trade and Industry backed report carried out by the British Bankers Association.

Training and Enterprise Councils, now succeeded by the Skills Councils, have undoubtedly done some fine work in bringing communities together, in a concerted effort to stimulate enterprise, boost employment opportunities, raise the level of competitiveness and educational standards.

From my vantage point, in observing the workings of the TEC movement, I was well placed, being as it were on the ground floor when it got off the ground, being one of the three directors who appointed our first Chief Executive for the North London TEC and attended meetings regularly.

North London TEC was fortunate in having a Board of high achievers who were committed to the task in hand. In many ways the TEC performance was spectacular in meeting targets and in the process several 'productivity' firsts for London, and at times for the country as a whole, were achieved.

But unfortunately, this performance miserably missed part of our brief. Large segments of ethnic businesses were excluded right under the noses of the Board. This was a sad indictment on the part of the TEC. How could this happen? There were three black board members and we took great care to act in the best interests of the whole constituency with a full board seal of approval.

What was to be discovered later was that agreeing policy at the top was one thing, but its implementation down the line was very much another matter. Critics might well say that control mechanisms available to the Board should have been in place to spot this weakness and there could be no disagreement about that.

Various suggestions as to how this matter might be resolved were discussed and eventually the Board ordered an independent outside investigation.

I was confident in my belief that understanding the problems and coming up with solutions was within the grasp and competence of the ethnic community itself. I therefore discussed my views with my chairman, Derek Wheeler, a very able secondment from Marks and Spencer, and suggested that he should look at the credentials of Statecraft Consultants, an ethnic business that itself was uniquely a by-product of the situation in which we found ourselves and whom I believed could deliver a solution.

Derek met with Rudi Page of Statecraft and was satisfied that he could deliver. The next step was to clear this with the Chief Executive of the TEC. He too was convinced and eventually the skills of Statecraft were brought in to deliver a solution by way of a strategy now known as 'Synergy' which found a fitting solution within the ethnic community itself.

The Synergy project had its conceptual origins in the TEC's acknowledgement that there were gaps in its services and activities as a major local economic agency, with the result that not all communities were reached or sufficiently involved in its activities or services. The need was subsequently identified by the NLTEC/BLLN board for a new operational framework for the brokerage and delivery of economic development services across the NLTEC area, that is, the London Boroughs of Barnet, Enfield and Haringey. Specifically the board recognised the need for a delivery mechanism that was not only professionally appropriate, but would additionally be seen as representative of the communities that were the key beneficiaries of the programme of services under consideration - in this case, the ethnic minority community. The Synergy project formally commenced in March 1999 when the NLTEC/BLLN appointed a project co-ordinator.

Earlier in February 1999, the NLTEC/BLLN had been similarly instrumental in the establishment of a public-private and not-for-profit partnership organisation with which the Synergy project would form a close working relationship. The North London Regional Dynamism conference held in June 1998, and the Synergy project, went on to become one of its key implementation tools. The stated aims of the NLCDF were for its membership to practice and promote equal opportunities in three key functional areas:

1. The recruitment and promotion of employees.
2. The treatment of customers and clients, and
3. The purchase and subcontracting of products and services.

The NLCDF membership included some of the largest employers in North London, the majority of which were public sector organisations, although its initial membership also included a number of organisations from the private, public and voluntary sectors.

Synergy has also often been cited by academics and practitioners alike as an example of a policy initiative with elements of good practice in it (see for example, NEF (New Economics Foundation) 2001; CEEDR (Centre for Enterprise and Economic Development Research) 2001; GLE (Greater London Eterprise) 2000.

The Synergy project has been a catalyst for making connections work between public, private and not-for-profit partnerships and has demonstrated its viability as a transferable working model that can be usefully employed by mainstream support providers where an effective communications strategy is considered beneficial as an implementation tool. For example, it's flexibility as a 'way of working' model is demonstrated in the three projects currently being worked on by the Synergy team using approaches originally developed for the Synergy project:

The Protocol Framework devised by Statecraft Consulting is an interlocking network of African, Caribbean and black British professionals, intermediaries and business owners that aims to support and enhance the membership's collective competitiveness by building on their collective management and entrepreneurial knowledge, skills and experience.

RCN Connect is a diversity, equality, and cultural understanding in representation and workforce support strategy developed for the Royal College of Nursing (West Midland Region) in terms of their outreach work, and in the area of communication of policies, procedures and guidelines.

(Barnet) Nexxus Project was commissioned by the Barnet Primary Care Trust, supported by the London Borough of Barnet, and is concerned with the development of a strategy for a joint health and regeneration approach to tackling business support and social exclusion issues in the London Borough of Barnet and the North London sub-region. It aims to deliver relevant advice, support and signposting through a series of concerted meetings, workshops, seminars and conferences underpinned by a targeted communication campaign.

In terms of the delivery of business support, one of the key issues that the Synergy approach demonstrated was its viability as a working model that could be usefully employed by mainstream business support providers for effective engagement with the ethnic minority business communities, if policy support is to make a real impact. The message of engagement is a resonant one, particularly for the recently established national Small Business Service (SBS), which has a brief to encourage and support entrepreneurship in all sections of society. Engagement is a necessary condition if this aim is to be achieved and to which other key principles may be added:

* A need to build on the acquired knowledge and experience of those business support providers who are skilled at working with EMBs.

* A need for an outreach strategy to engage EMB's, along with more traditional promotional approaches such as advertising via target media;

* A need for ethnic minority business representation across the structures set up to manage the Small Business Service and such other institutions;

* A need for mechanisms to enable dialogue between EMB's and other stakeholders and policy makers on an on-going basis.

A need for the SBS to establish procedures and practices to facilitate effective implementation of the engagement strategy. These should include the recruitment and retention of additional ethnic minority advisors; cultural awareness training for all business advisors operating in areas with potential EMB clients; establishing appropriate EMB targets together with effective procedures to monitoring their achievement; taking a wider approach to supply chain development which includes enabling large purchasers to adopt supplier diversity measures.

Clearly, however, the ultimate success for Synergy or similar projects would be to eliminate the need for such projects by integrating their objectives into the mainstream infrastructure.

Initiating the process that led to "*Synergy*" is a good example of influencing change. For me this has been immensely gratifying and a credit to everyone in making a solution possible, in particular, Rudi Page of Statecraft Consulting.

Our diversity is a major strength, and it is within this rich cultural mix, that we must influence meaningful change and release its full potential to interact and relate with the rest of the world.

Meaningful change, will only take place if all the parties concerned work hard to influence it.

The Department of Trade and Industry has it in its power to incorporate the machinery to influence change by setting guidelines and conditions of accountability for their main contractors that shows and demonstrates how its sub contracts take into account inclusiveness in their distribution of work in the depressed inner urban areas.

In an effort to get the Afro-Caribbean community seriously moving into the business of wealth creation, the failed methods of funding need to be re-examined. The DTI should consider and examine a set-aside directed at businesses in growth areas and remove the drip feed principle through the same old channels, which have not penetrated the core needs of the community.

Funding through a rethink of some elements of the Loan Guarantee Scheme is another possible route, but making the banks comply in co-operating this time round. This course of action will send a boosting signal of confidence to the business community.

It's not only governments that must initiate change, big business has a central role to play by taking their corporate responsibility seriously in providing training opportunities for suitable candidates by way of mentoring or secondment where there is no conflict of interest.

Another suggestion might well be to test the willingness of our financial institutions to put together a contributory revolving fund put at the disposal of medium sized expanding businesses. This is a role that could well be filled by the venture capital companies.

We are a great nation, with London, a world class city, a knowledge based financial hub, attracting as it does, business people with creative drive and energy, and among these are ethnic people, who ask only to be accorded nothing more than equal opportunity.

The unstinted support of our financial institutions must be encouraged to stand squarely behind those with creative and energetic drive.

The above suggestions are challenges for central government, leadership by the captains of industry and our financial institutions.

Let us look at the valiant efforts in South London, which might well be the model for communities working in harmony together.

Brixton's place in contemporary black British history and its influence on change in 2003 are positively encouraging.

Visiting Windrush Square on Friday 16th May, that marks the birth place of the Windrush Generation, was for me a day that strengthened my faith and belief in the black community's will to succeed, contribute, add value and signpost its direction with an assured confidence that is well routed.

I dropped in first at a Natwest bank to see what I would find. There was a majority of smiling black faces behind the counter dishing out the cash, while a steady stream of customers were lining up for service.

I popped in and out of a number of the well-branded stores and found a similar pattern that big companies are beginning to value diversity and realise the importance of inclusiveness.

A sample check of people placement in the management structure of the organisations was also an important indicator of progressive change. At

Boots I spoke with Mrs. N. Meghyi, store manager, who spoke candidly about her satisfaction of her place in the organisation and who saw the future positively. At Woolworth, Jason Sardinah, the general manager, was also of ethnic stock and below him four middle managers. At J. Sainsbury's I found Jonathan Cookson as general manager, with Jonathan Baker as floor manager, while at W H Smith the general manager was Aubrey David, also of ethnic stock, whereas at Marks and Spencer there were a number of black section managers.

My next stop was 378 Coldharbour Lane, home of AMBH (Archives and Museum of Black Heritage), a project of Black Cultural Archives funded by the Heritage Lottery Fund. I was greeted warmly by Sam Walker, Director of the project.

There could not be a more fitting home for a Monument to the past and for the future than Brixton. Wandering around the Museum fills one with a sense of pride and dignity. The Museum's 2002 August-December newsletter makes the all important points that our community must constantly be aware of. (Talking about documenting and collecting Black British cultural and social history is one thing, but providing a home to act as a repository for this re-valued material evidence that will represent generations of contributions to the life of British Society is something of a bigger challenge. Connecting the Windrush Generations of the 1940s and 50s with the twenty first and three centuries earlier of Black presence in Britain is but one of the primary aims of the African Peoples Monument Foundation).

Hats off to our leaders with the vision. It remains the duty of each of us to do our bit in making our presence and contribution an indelible mark on British Society.

Great music and entertainment is part of the rich and fascinating culture to be found in Brixton and with that in mind I dropped into the Music Box on Coldharbour Lane and spoke to Fethaint Hakin, the store manager, a stunningly beautiful black young lady. My curiosity about her name led me to enquire about her origins. "I am Norwegian", she giggled. "And why Brixton?" I enquired. "There is no Brixton in Norway" she said, "and there is nowhere else quite like Brixton" she told me, which sums it all up.

On rounding off my day in Brixton, I tried to find out what made Brixtonians tick. In almost every answer, it was the friendliness of its people, a resoluteness to influence change, to make things happen, and in the process, Brixton is on a roll, a fast moving vibrant place, positively celebrating its diversity.

Music

Black people enjoy music, and are good at it. This is a cliché as deep-rooted as our penchant for sport. However, lack of recognition and more so acknowledgement of our great contribution to this art form, has frustrated many in our community, while attitudes outside the community have been rigid. Yet African Caribbean people have developed different styles of music which are popular world-wide. In this industry, our impact is disproportionate or uneven to our actual numbers. The 1994/95 edition of the Pears Encyclopaedia published our universal dominance in this industry, through a defined range of performers, song-writers, arrangers and other musical talent that our community is richly endowed with.

A particular melody, note or type of music, brings a feeling of nostalgia. Little wonder that the earlier immigrants, who were cold, alone and a long way from home, found solace in Caribbean music. In the late 1950s, calypso was fashionable, inspired by the American actor and singer, Harry Belafonte, anther son of the region. His was not the real thing and only served to increase the desire to produce, or somehow provide our own music.

Sections of the indigenous population were surprised at the different musical tastes enjoyed by each Caribbean territory and its citizens. The Jamaicans for instance were not too keen on steelband music, while Trinidadians adore it. In those early days, reggae was not on the music scene. I understand that Mento was the main style in Jamaica, but it has come to the end of its popularity in those days and it could not cross over musically to Britain. In fact West Indians who came to Britain in the ten to fifteen years after the Second World war, were influenced by the American Rhythm 'n' Blues records. Fats Domino and Chuck Berry were very popular, as well as the little known Johnny Ace and Shirley & Lee. Gospel Queen, Mahalia Jackson, with her dynamic spirituals energised the community at all levels. Most were amazed that such brilliant artistes were not of West Indian origin, although Belafonte could have claimed his roots in the region. Indeed, this period was a true reflection of what is often described as the Golden Oldies era - a time in which Nat King Cole, Charlie Pride, Louis 'Satchmo' Armstrong, Count Basie, Ella Fitzgerald, amongst others, held the spotlight in the world of music.

Caribbean music was not played on radio or television, and frequent house parties across England, organised by individuals or groups of West Indians, were used to channel information on new (record) releases and other developments in the Caribbean music industry. The first set of records were brought to Britain by 'new arrivals' from the Caribbean or by visitors passing through from the US. Some of the young ladies received records from their GI boyfriends.

By the 1960's, the importation of records increased considerably. Trinidadians Lord Kitchener, the Mighty Sparrow and Lord Melody were amongst the calypsonians most frequently listened to by the community. Kitchener resided in Britain for some time. Wilfred Edwards and Owen Gray - both Jamaicans - who are still going strong, made a name for themselves in the Caribbean music industry and impacted on their community, especially during the formative years.

The small Blue Beat label tried to blend the best of Jamaica with the first records made from the talent in Britain. By combining Prince Buster with Laurel Aitken, this label was the name applied to a whole style of music. As the American influence waned in the 1960s, it seemed that there was great excitement, enthusiasm and talent waiting to explode. And it did.

Millie Small provided that release. Young, attractive and lively, her My Boy Lollipop was bouncy and catchy. Although her lyrical composition was somewhat nonsensical, the song was top of the charts in 1964. Millie could not repeat a similar success, but she established a landmark, proving to the English and the international pop music community, the vast potential of African Caribbean musical talent.

Island Records, owned by Chris Blackwell, a rich man with Jamaican connections, exploited the opportunities to the full. In time, his company expanded from a specialist ethnic function into a major world-wide enterprise handling many of the stars of the industry. Within weeks of My Boy Lollipop, many of the top singers of the West Indies came to Britain to advance their careers. They found too late, that at this time, it was only a passing phase. The national market turned soon to other interests - it was the heyday of 'Beatlemania'. The African Caribbean community did not have the organisational structure to place its cultural entertainment talent on a professional footing. In such circumstances, therefore, the evolution of our market had to be more gradual.

The Palmer brothers from north-west London were among the pioneers to give a boost to young artistes in Britain, by allowing them to perform music which was popular in the US. By operating the Apollo Club in Willesden, the Palmers provided a live outlet for visiting singers and other entertainers to market their records. There was a better framework for accommodating the second bout of energetic talent at the end of the 60s. Desmond Dekker showed similar characteristics to Millie in making Israelites, a major international hit. His heavy Jamaican accent seemed ideally suited for the new-styled Ska tradition. There were so many artistes of quality that two Caribbean Music Festivals were presented at Wembley Arena during this period. Jimmy Cliff, the Pioneers, Ken Booth, John Holt, Bob and Marcia, who captured the feeling of the times with 'Young Gifted and Black', ensured that there were sufficient hits to render the African Caribbean musical presence a permanent feature of British society. Later, English pop star, Boy George developed a self-contained industry linked with similar communities in Africa, the West Indies and the US.

Reggae is the mode of music which is associated with Jamaica and by implication, the people of African Caribbean descent. Robert 'Bob' Nesta Marley became a superstar by the 1970's and his popularity intensified following his premature death in 1981. His vibrant personality was matched by his unique method of delivery and identification with Rastafarianism. His music developed a rich cultural and visual dimension based on its own traditional rhythm. His great albums - *Exodus*, *Rastaman Vibration*, *Kaie* and his songs, *No Woman No Cry*, *Songs of Freedom* and *War* - all symbolised universal greatness and a philosophy in the oneness of Man. He stamped his authority on the music scene in Africa, the Caribbean, Europe, North America and wherever peace-loving people gathered. If Marley was alive, he would still be revered as an equal to the Mighty Sparrow (King of Calypso), Michael Jackson (King of Pop) and Arrow (King of Soca).

The generation of interest in and formation of a new industry which originated primarily in the Jamaican experience, was to the benefit also of musicians from the Eastern Caribbean. When Soca was born from the fusion of Soul and Calypso Montserratian, Arrow, drew a huge following to his live performances in the United Kingdom, North America and Western Europe. Top performers from Africa - Fela Kuti and King Sunny Ade - made successful tours to Britain as well.

The movement was not only one way. Instead of artistes coming to London from the Caribbean, there was a reverse in this trend. New technologies in music was an added advantage for composers, lyricists, producers and arrangers. Musical artistes and groups travelled to the Caribbean to impart their skills to their counterparts.

Guyanese Eddie Grant came into the musical limelight in the 1960s with the Equals, who also included his brothers - Rudy and Alpine. In later years Eddie developed a career as an accomplished singer, producer and businessman, with his company Ice Records. At one time, many felt he had become the natural successor to Marley, but at the peak of his fame, Grant migrated from London to his new home in Barbados.

By the middle of the 1980s, the scope of music had transcended all boundaries of cultural, social and traditional values. Joan Armatrading's songs appealed to audiences of all races universally. Joan grew up in the West Midlands and wrote songs based on her experiences. Her compositions were distinctive, without belonging to any specially defined genre.

Five Star may not have attained the status of the Jacksons, but they have provided ample evidence that Britain can produce a well polished, professional act with a brilliant visual impact. They are a quintet of brothers and sisters whose father and manager, Buster Pearson, was a guitarist with the Links in the 1960s. The latter laid the foundation for the contemporary music industry while the quintet provided support for visiting Americans.

Professionally, there was hardly any difference between Five Star and the Americans and English of similar kind. Today in Britain, black enterprise in popular music forms is distinguished from other traditional art forms. There are some media and methods which cannot be anything other than African Caribbean.

The credit for this sound should be given to the many unknown technicians fiddling away until they get it right, in make-shift studios throughout the community, as well as to the more celebrated producers. As a people we have always been good at putting things together with our hands, and it is not surprising that some of the first independent business ventures were in car maintenance and in producing music.

Artists of West Indian descent who attained national fame are not necessarily popular in their community. That is due to the method of compiling statistics from sales at a selection of shops mainly in large city centres. The African Caribbean music scene is conducted, like so many businesses, on a more localised basis, even though the network of independent local activities covers the greater part of the country.

The presence of (blasting) sound systems at parties, fairs and at various festivals, including the annual carnival festivities, is another feature of black music enterprise in Britain. These sound systems were first introduced at house parties or small community centres and church halls to attract support. There is often competition to determine which system is best. These mobile systems are taken on visits to other towns or to the seaside. They are very popular at night clubs - some with a lifespan of little more than a couple of weeks, while others have a tradition of many years. This addition to the vocal instrumentation of music is clearly suited for the present generation. However, despite their popularity, it would be unwise to favour any for special mention in this chapter.

Another musical pioneer who held is own was William Campbell, also known as 'Count Suckle'. He gained recognition by his sound system as Columbo's in Soho. Then in the mid-1960s, he founded the Cue Club in Paddington. His customers comprised American servicemen, visitors and the local community. Former world heavyweight boxing champion, Muhammad Ali, was among his many distinguished guests who frequented the club.

Because the normal channels were closed to them, or were too expensive for local appeal and modest budgets, African Caribbean record companies turned increasingly to the independent pirate radio stations. By saturating a restricted area, these programmes encouraged a regular supply of new talent but by their nature, have not assisted them to develop beyond that level.

There is still no national recording industry as such. The lines of communication from the Caribbean are reggae from Jamaica, Soca from the Eastern Caribbean and Salsa from Latin America/Caribbean. Aitken and Gray have retained their popularity in the provinces long after they faded from public attention in London.

The various attempts to build a Jamaican Sunsplash equivalent in Britain have been unsuccessful. Public concerts in open parks attract large crowds without establishing their own tradition. It was inevitable that all shows taking place in the summer months embraced the Notting Hill Carnival, an event that commands international recognition, respect and support. It is a vital part of our enterprise culture that we must uphold with dignity and pride.

The idea of creating the Trinidadian Carnival in London can be traced back to activist and publisher Claudia Jones in the early 1960s, but credit is usually given to Leslie Palmer for rescheduling the event in the summer when weather conditions are more conducive. The festivities have grown substantially - with the numbers of participants, revellers and spectators - not forgetting extensive media attention. In short, it has been a great success.

The greatest problem with Carnival is that much is expected from the event. The traditional festivities in Port-of-Spain have been blended with those associated with Jamaican independence and Sunsplash, which occur at about the same time.

Nevertheless, the Caribbean Carnival is spread over three cities in three weeks. It has already expanded in Birmingham and Leicester, while smaller events are held in various inner city boroughs including the City of London.

Carnival tells us something more important about black enterprise than music itself. The festival has spawned its own cultural industries: cottage, costume manufacturing, food and drinks, the performing arts, media advertising and publishing. It is one of the few activities in which time, effort and other (cultural) resources are richly invested in children.

In the last few years, cultural industries have become part of the European Social Fund criteria, and bearing in mind that black people still have a stranglehold on the world of music (like sports), it is high time to take advantage of such a prestigious position and continue to set our own agenda in this sphere of industry.

WEST INDIAN STANDING CONFERENCE

The West Indian Standing Conference
5 Westminster Bridge Road
London SE1 7XW

Telephone: 020-7928-7861/2
Fax: 020-7928-0343
E-Mail: wiscorgan@aol.com

Britain's Longest Serving Black Organisation
Founded 1958 and providing
Continuous Service to the Black Community

About the WISC:
WISC is an umbrella organisation, which was formed in 1968 to promote the
interests of the Afro-Caribbean community in Britain. Over the years, it has been the
forefront of the Afro-Caribbean people's campaign for improved conditions of justice
and equality of opportunity.

- FREE LEGAL ADVICE & COUNSELLING
- WHAT WE DO: WE PROVIDE DIRECT SERVICES TO MEMBER
  GROUPS AND INDIVIDUALS IN THE COMMUNITY.
- NETWORKING IN THE COMMUNITY

The conference analyse central and local government policies and the
effects on the African Caribbean voluntary sector and make information
accessible to the African Caribbean voluntary sector.